Women
Who Knew
Paul

Zacchaeus Studies: New Testament

General Editor: Mary Ann Getty

Women
Who Knew
Paul

Florence M. Gillman

A Michael Glazier Book
THE LITURGICAL PRESS
Collegeville, Minnesota

A Michael Glazier Book published by The Liturgical Press.

Cover design by David Manahan, O.S.B. Detail of fresco "Scenes from the Lives of St. Stephen and St. Lawrence" by Fra Angelico, 1455, Vatican Museum.

2	3	4	5	6	7	8	9

Library of Congress Cataloging-in-Publication Data

Gillman, Florence Morgan.
    Women who knew Paul / by Florence Morgan Gillman.
        p.   cm.
    Includes bibliographical references.
    ISBN 0-8146-5674-9
    1. Women in the Bible. 2. Church history—Primitive and early church, ca. 30–600. 3. Paul, the Apostle, Saint—Relations with women. 4. Bible. N.T. Epistles of Paul—Criticism, interpretation, etc. 5. Bible. N.T. Acts—Criticism, interpretation, etc. I. Title.
BS2655.W5G54 1991
225.9'22'082—dc20   91-7647
                                             CIP

*This book is gratefully dedicated
to the women whose lives have most shaped mine,
my mother, Ann, my grandmothers, Mary and Vergie,
to the man who is my treasured companion,
my husband, John,
and to our little daughter, Anne Marie.*

Contents

Acknowledgments

The research for this book was partially funded by a National Endowment for the Humanities Travel to Collections grant which enabled me to visit and use the resources of Mullen Library, The Catholic University of America. Much of the writing of the text was made possible and influenced by my participation in a National Endowment for the Humanities Summer Seminar for College Teachers, "The Sociology of Early Christianity," directed by Howard Clark Kee at Boston University, summer 1986.

I wish also to acknowledge the continued encouragement for my study of Paul which has come from my mentor, Prof. Jan Lambrecht, S.J., and from Prof. Raymond F. Collins, both of the Faculty of Theology, Catholic University of Louvain.

Special thanks goes to my husband and colleague, John, for his collaboration in the research for this manuscript, his careful reading of the text, and his helpful comments and suggestions.

Editor's Note

Zacchaeus Studies provide concise, readable and relatively inexpensive scholarly studies on particular aspects of scripture and theology. The New Testament section of the series presents studies dealing with focal or debated questions; and the volumes focus on specific texts or particular themes of current interest in biblical interpretation. Specialists have their professional journals and other forums where they discuss matters of mutual concern, exchange ideas and further contemporary trends of research; and some of their work on contemporary biblical research is now made accessible for students and others in *Zacchaeus Studies*.

The authors in this series share their own scholarship in nontechnical language, in the areas of their expertise and interest. These writers stand with the best in current biblical scholarship in the English-speaking world. Since most of them are teachers, they are accustomed to presenting difficult material in comprehensible form without compromising a high level of critical judgment and analysis.

The works of this series are ecumenical in content and purpose and cross credal boundaries. They are designed to augment formal and informal biblical study and discussion. Hopefully they will also serve as texts to enhance and supplement seminary, university and college classes. The series will also aid Bible study groups, adult education and parish religious education classes to develop intelligent, versatile and challenging programs for those they serve.

Mary Ann Getty
New Testament Editor

Introduction

Famous people tend to travel down through the pages of history accompanied by an entourage of other characters, most of whose stories, were it not for the famed person, would not otherwise have been remembered. Such is the case with the Apostle Paul and many of those whose lives touched on his.[1] Apart from the few New Testament sources which contain information about Paul (his own letters,[2] the Deutero-Pauline letters, and the Acts of the Apostles), the history of Christian origins would not even know the names of such people as Prisca and Aquila, Apollos, Phoebe, Lydia, Silas, Timothy, and a host of others. Ironically, in studying Paul these characters emerge as so fascinating in themselves, that one begins to wish, without taking an ounce away from Paul's own significance, to move him out of the center of attention for a time in an attempt to know the others better.

Of all the Pauline characters who attract our curiosity, a high degree of interest is currently directed toward the women with whom Paul interacted: his relatives, friends, acquaintances, coworkers, converts, and political contacts. This is understandable given contemporary Church struggles involving the justice issues

---

[1]On persons associated with Paul see esp. F. F. Bruce, *The Pauline Circle* (Grand Rapids: Eerdmans, 1985).

[2]Herein assumed to be 1 Thessalonians, Galatians, 1–2 Corinthians, Romans, Philippians, and Philemon.

of sexism and patriarchalism. These concerns cause much attention to be focussed on the Pauline Churches since they are the
subject of such a large segment of the New Testament material
on earliest Christianity, and also because of Paul's tendency to
make statements about women (cf. e.g., Gal 3:28; 1 Cor 7;
11:2-16; 14:33b-36), some of which later Christianity has relied
upon to enforce the unjust subordination of women to men in
both society and Church.

The women who knew Paul are also of much interest today
to scholars whose concern it is to reconstruct the earliest history
of Christianity more fully than has hitherto been done. For those
involved in this enterprise the widespread awareness that our very
New Testament sources betray a male perspective and bias, and
thus tend to trivialize if not ignore and bury the history of women,
has led to an attempt to extract as fully as possible whatever information about women remains to be gleaned from the extant
documents.[3]

All of this has resulted in a heightened curiosity about the actual
women whose lives intersected with Paul's. Who were they? What
were their lives like? What did they think about their world and
their religious situation? What did they think about Paul? While
only a few of these women's names are recorded and only scattered details survive about their lives, they intrigue us by their
very existence. How interesting it would be to know them well,
to be able to question them at length, to listen to them tell their
stories. Certainly we would thereby more fully understand the
great Paul, whose legacy to Christianity is unquestionably mas-
sive. But of major importance, we would also better know a group
of women whose lives in their own right also touched upon or
affected the shaping of early Christianity. As they emerge from
Paul's shadow, these women would confront us with interesting
and challenging life stories of their own.

"Paul's shadow," however, is the great problem in any study
of the women who knew him. For, those who come to us as his
entourage in history come precisely in his wake. This is so, first,
because the New Testament sources in which they are mentioned
focus primarily on Paul. But, secondly, in post-New Testament
interpretative literature, the women, more so than the men who

---

[3]See e.g., Elisabeth Schüssler Fiorenza, *In Memory of Her. A Feminist Reconstruction
of Christian Origins* (New York: Crossroad, 1983) 43-95.

knew Paul, have been relegated to greater obscurity (e.g., the deacon Phoebe has been reduced to being a deaconess or helper),
even erasure (e.g., Junia, Nympha, and Syntyche have been taken
to be males; Damaris was deleted from some editions) by many
biblical commentators whose own cultural or ecclesiastical perspectives made it impossible for them to acknowledge, or even
to entertain objectively, the actual significance or roles some of
these women quite obviously had.

The intention in this short study is to bring some of the women
who knew Paul out of his shadow by introducing and describing
them as fully as the limited literary sources will allow. Attention
will be given primarily to the various, often minute, details the
epistles and Acts include about these people.[4] When possible an
effort will be made to draw out the implications of those details
with respect to each woman's life situation. Some non-literary
sources (such as described below) are also brought into the discussion. The result is a series of partial sketches, extremely uneven in length and in the breadth of aspects of a person's life which
are touched upon. This is, of course, due to the different types
and amount of detail available to relate to each woman.

It must be kept in mind that the literary materials which link
these women with Paul are of two types: there are primary sources,
i.e., Paul's own letters, in which it is assumed the information
given is historically accurate; there are also secondary sources,
i.e., the Deutero-Pauline letters and Acts, all of which were written in the post-Pauline decades. While the persons mentioned in
the secondary sources very possibly reflect a historical link with
Paul in the traditions passed on about the apostle, nevertheless
they and their actions may reflect the editing, or even creation,
by the authors of those texts. Our approach in the use of these
secondary sources has been to assume the historicity of persons
mentioned as far as possible.[5]

---

[4] While the final chapter relies upon Acts, it depends even more upon the writings
of Josephus.

[5] Cf. F. F. Bruce, "The Acts of the Apostles Today," *Bulletin of the John Rylands
Library* 65 (1982) 36–56, 56, whose survey of the interpretation of Acts concludes there
are now "indications that the study of this important book is emerging from a generation of unnecessary scepticism and entering a new phase in which its value is better
appreciated as a trustworthy source for our knowledge of the history as well as the
theology of primitive Christianity."

We must also remind ourselves that in the case of both the letters and Acts[6] the documents are written by men reflecting what *they* thought about various matters; the texts do not offer women's perceptions about anything. Thus, to learn these women's stories, or to try to see things from their viewpoint, a shift in emphasis away from that found in the literature must be attempted. The women need somehow to be placed in the center of the camera's lens. For that reason, for example, we purposely refer to them as the "women who knew Paul," not "women known by Paul." The first phrasing is chosen since it implies that Paul also came into their lives, not just they into his. Each woman is thus viewed as her own center of gravity, not merely as a participant in the dramatic events of Paul's life. Unfortunately for any reconstruction of their stories, however, the texts from which our information comes are overwhelmingly centered on Paul.

Shifting the focus onto these women also means that the perspectives of Paul and other men need to be balanced with women's perspectives. Bernadette Brooten has noted in this respect, however, that methodologically putting women in center place means that "the caterories developed to understand the history of man may no longer be accurate, that the traditional historical periods and canons of literature may not be the proper framework, and that we will need to ask new types of questions and consider hitherto overlooked sources."[7]

This observation reflects the growing recognition among scholars that the study of early Christian women is not parallel to the study of early Christian men. The existing literary sources, for the most part, relegate women merely to the backdrop. Thus there is a radical lack of knowledge about females in early Christianity, as well as throughout antiquity. To describe this situation concerning how little we know about first century C.E. women, Brooten brings in the term "prehistory," one she gets from Mary

---

[6]This is obviously true also for the writings of Josephus to which reference will likewise be made.

[7]Bernadette Brooten, "Early Christian Women and Their Cultural Context: Issues of Method in Historical Reconstruction," in Adela Yarbro Collins (ed.), *Feminist Perspectives on Biblical Scholarship,* SBL Centennial Publications 10 (Chico, CA: Scholars Press, 1985) 65–91, 65. On methodology, see also Elisabeth Schüssler Fiorenza, "Missionaries, Apostles, Coworkers: Romans 16 and the Reconstruction of Women's Early Christian History," *Word and World* 6 (1986) 420–433, 420–423.

Daly.[8] Brooten uses this term to describe this era of women's history. It denotes that knowledge about women is almost entirely missing; only a comparatively few scattered fragments have been preserved.

Yet to speak of early Christian women as embedded in prehistory is not to say that the quest to get to know them better is hopeless. Again, to quote Brooten, should we give up we would be "letting those who have erased women from history have the last say."[9] Nevertheless, to speak of the women who knew Paul as being in prehistory is to recognize that reconstructing their stories is a task in which the resources used are akin to those drawn upon in assembling the history of both men and women from ages more conventionally termed prehistory, such as the Stone Age. In other words, the limitation of our literary sources, mainly by men about men, and only here and there about women requires also bringing into play other usually overlooked sources. These might include, for example, non-literary documents in the form of inscriptions or papyri, archaeological data, remains of monuments, art, funeral remains along with, of course, the few literary sources which do allude to women.[10]

As with any study of prehistory, however, reconstructing early Christian women's stories cannot escape a tentativeness which comes from having to employ much speculation, even imagination. A mirror image or photograph of women's lives is, in the end, not possible. At best, an artist's sketch is produced. This may seem less exact than the more so-called objective claims which are often assumed, if not expressly made, in historical reconstructions about men. Paul himself serves as an example. Details about his life appear to be abundant in contrast to what can be pieced together about the women whose lives touched his. Yet, given that the literary sources about Paul represent only a male view of reality, even lengthy, detailed reconstructions of Paul based on the

---

[8]See Brooten "Early Christian Women," 67. She cites from Mary Daly, *Gyn/Ecology. The Metaethics of Radical Feminism* (Boston: Beacon, 1978) 24.

[9]Brooten, "Early Christian Women," 67.

[10]A significant example of an analysis which tries to reconstruct the lives and thinking of certain women on the basis of such a broad spectrum of evidence is Lilian Portefaix's *Sisters Rejoice. Paul's Letter to the Philippians and Luke-Acts as Received by First-Century Philippian Women.* Coniectanea Biblica NT Series 20 (Uppsala: Almqvist and Wiksell International, 1988).

male perspectives of those texts are in the end highly tentative, partial sketches.

The knowledge that the history of Christian origins is distorted with respect to both men's and women's stories by the very nature of the documents at our disposal leaves us with a challenge to overcome that distortion to whatever extent is possible. With respect to the women who knew Paul, perhaps studies such as this take a step in that direction. It is important, however, to stress that we concentrate here on only one aspect of examining early Christian women's lives, namely, literary references to these people. In that sense it is hoped that the readers of this text, especially the college and adult Bible students for whom it is especially intended, will use this as a gateway to the broad spectrum of information which must be brought to play in the study of the women of the early Churches.

The reader will note that the women examined in this study are variously grouped on a thematic basis rather than being treated as all the Philippian or Roman or Corinthian women together.[11] Thus we will look at them as Paul's family members, as Christians noted for their faith, as members of Churches some of whom held the specific role or characterization of deacon, apostle, co-worker, worker in the Lord, prophet and sister, and as women with distinct social roles such as household heads and political figures. This type of thematic arrangement was chosen with the hope that our survey might offer information not only about these specific women but also allow their life stories to function for the modern observer as types. The thirty or so women described can only be but a fraction of those whose lives had an impact upon early Christianity. But, through them we can glean a bit of insight into the much larger crowd. These individuals are probably reminiscent of others who were drawn to the early Church or who were among its leaders and members. Their stories thus are not merely their own but suggestive echoes of many others who played a role in the drama of nascent Christianity, yet who remain buried in obscurity.

---

[11]The grouping is not intended to be exclusive; some of the women obviously could fit into more than one of the categories. For a perspective on some of these women grouped on a regional basis, see e.g. my "Early Christian Women at Philippi," *Journal of Gender in World Religions* 1 (1990) 59–79.

1

Women in Paul's Family

Of the various women whose lives touched upon Paul's, those we would naturally like to analyze first are the ones we suspect would have had much early influence upon him. These include his mother, any sisters, and his wife if he were married. While Paul himself makes no direct reference to these women and they remain essentially unknown to us, a few points can be brought up for discussion.

Paul does say concerning his background that he was "of the people of Israel, of the tribe of Benjamin, a Hebrew born of Hebrews" (Phil 3:5; cf. Acts 21:39; 22:3). From this it may be concluded that both of his parents were Jewish, more specifically, Benjaminites, and that his designation of them as Hebrews indicates they had retained their ancestral languages (Aramaic in the home; Hebrew in the synagogue) in the Greek-speaking city of Tarsus where they lived and where Paul was born. To have kept their native tongue would have been a sign of strict adherence to their familial culture. It could also have meant that they had emigrated relatively recently from Palestine and still preserved their Palestinian ways, unlike other Tarsian Jews who were more thoroughly assimilated. Jerome, writing in the fourth century C.E., does say that Paul's parents were originally from the region of Gischala, thus from Galilee.[1] But Jerome's source for this information is unknown, and the lateness of the tradition casts suspicion on its reliability. Thus, overall there is little which can be

---

[1] Jerome, *Liber de viris illustribus*, 5 (*PL* 23, col. 646); *Com. in Ep. ad Philemon*, 23 (*PL* 26, col. 653).

said about Paul's mother other than that she must have been a Jewess, a Benjaminite, and still able to use her ancestral languages even as she lived in the Diaspora, where she had to be conversant with Greek also.

According to Acts 21:39 and 22:27, Paul held both Tarsian and Roman citizenship. This suggests his parents had achieved a rather privileged civic status. How they had done so is a matter of some speculation. Admission to the roll of citizenship in Tarsus is known to have been by a property qualification.[2] As for the greater privilege of Roman citizenship, however, how it came to them is not known. The fact that Luke says Paul was a tentmaker (Acts 18:3), and the likelihood that he must have learned his trade from his parents[3] have led to the not improbable theory that Paul's family had supplied the Romans with tents at a time of pressing need and been rewarded with citizenship.[4]

If Paul did in fact come from a family of tentmakers, the question arises as to his mother's role in the business. That couples worked together at tentmaking is suggested by Acts when both Prisca and Aquila seem to be designated as tentmakers (cf. 18:3: ". . . by trade they were tentmakers"). Ronald Hock, however, doubts that Prisca worked alongside her husband. He reasons that "had tents been a product of weavers [rather than leatherworkers, as is widely held], the likelihood would be better, since weaving was often, though not exclusively, a woman's trade."[5] Nevertheless, such an observation is highly generalized. The phrasing of Acts 18:3 causes us to continue to entertain the possibility that Prisca, and by extension therefore a person such as Paul's mother, worked along with their husbands in their family tentmaking shops.[6]

As for Paul's early developmental years and his mother's influence upon him, there is almost no data. The only direct reference to that period is recorded in Acts 22:3 where the Lukan Paul

---

[2]See F. F. Bruce, *Paul. Apostle of the Heart Set Free* (Grand Rapids: Eerdmans, 1977) 34–36.

[3]So Ronald Hock, *The Social Context of Paul's Ministry* (Philadelphia: Fortress, 1980) 22–25.

[4]See Bruce, *Paul,* 37, who cites this as a suggestion made to him by Sir William Calder.

[5]Hock, *Context,* 81, n. 46.

[6]See below, p. 51.

states that he was brought up in Jerusalem at the feet of Gamaliel, "educated according to the strict manner of the law of our fathers." Unfortunately this statement does not specify at how early an age Paul was sent to Jerusalem nor does it explain why.

Because Paul never mentions his mother (nor his father), it has been conjectured either that his parents died before Paul became a follower of Jesus, thus before the period of his extant letters, or that his family disowned him because of his post-Damascus Road activity.[7] While neither theory can be tested, the latter seems less probable since Acts 23:16 refers to a tradition that Paul had a nephew, his sister's son, who late in Paul's travels, came to his aid in Jerusalem. This sole New Testament reference to Paul's sister tells nothing about her except to imply that through her son she remained in contact with Paul. It is not evident whether she or her son lived in Jerusalem or whether he was a visitor or a resident there.

Nothing further is known about Paul's sister. Nor can more be said about Paul's mother and his relationship to her, except perhaps to note that, assumably because of her, Paul had a true appreciation of a mother-child bond. This led him to greet a woman for whom he held great affection, the mother of Rufus, as his mother also (Rom 16:13).[8] While it is not evident what Paul means when he speaks thus of the mother of Rufus, it is generally understood that she was not his natural mother. One suggestion is that she may have extended her patronage to Paul.[9]

As nebulous as details are about Paul's mother and sister, whether he had a wife is a matter about which there is even less knowledge. If Paul did marry, he must have done so before his conversion since he indicates in 1 Corinthians 9:5 that he was not accompanied by a wife during his apostolic travels. Paul's charge in 1 Corinthians 7:8, "To the unmarried and the widows I say that it is well for them to remain single as I do," allows for the possibility that Paul was either unmarried or a widower. C. K. Barrett has noted, Paul "may never have married; it is however

[7]See William Ramsay, *St. Paul the Traveller and the Roman Citizen* (London: Hodder and Stoughton, 14th ed. 1920) 35–36; 310–312.

[8]On the mother of Rufus, see below, p. 74.

[9]So Wayne Meeks, *The First Urban Christians. The Social World of the Apostle Paul* (New Haven: Yale University Press, 1983) 60.

more probable that he was a widower. Unmarried rabbis were few, and marriage appears to have been obligatory for a Jewish man . . ., though one cannot suppose that this rule was universally observed."[10] Even if Paul was married, however, all details of the woman whose life may have been bonded to his elude us.[11]

In summary, the domestic and familial side of Paul's relationships with women remains quite obscure. Apart from the few points we have noted about his mother and her life in Tarsus, the presence of his sister in Jerusalem, and the possibility that he had a wife, it is with disappointment that one turns away from any hoped for closer acquaintance with Paul's female relatives. Fortunately, investigations of some of the other women who knew Paul allow for somewhat more expansive encounters.

[10]C. K. Barrett, *The First Epistle to the Corinthians.* Black's New Testament Commentaries (London: Black, 2nd. ed. 1971) 161.

[11]The theory that the person referred to enigmatically as "Yokefellow" in Philippians 4:3 (RSV: "my fellow worker") is actually Lydia of Philippi to whom Paul had "yoked" himself in marriage has nothing to support it. See below, p. 46.

2

Remembered for Their Faith:
Lois and Eunice, Damaris

To be recorded "accidentally" in history, that is, to be remembered primarily in function of someone else, is to be put in a possibly compromising position. One might become known for events or characteristics that are not at all central to one's life. This would have been true, for example, if Paul and Barnabas were known solely in function of John Mark and mentioned in relation to him just because they disagreed about taking him along on their travels (cf. Acts 15:36–39). Or, if all that the New Testament said about Paul were written in relation to Peter, i.e. that Paul had had a public argument with him in Antioch (cf. Gal 2:11-21), again we would have a very limited impression of Paul. He would go down in history primarily as confrontative. How narrow a slice of life to be remembered for!

Many of the New Testament women are in an analogous situation. They get mentioned briefly, usually in function of someone else, and are thus memorialized in early Christianity due to only a bit of accidental information. Happily for some, tradition's minimal preservation of details at least touches on a truly integral aspect of life. Examples of such women are those recalled for their faith. So it is with Lois and Eunice. They are mentioned in 2 Timothy 1:5 because of their relationship to Timothy and thus their connection with Paul, but characterized in that linking as women of great faith. Likewise with Damaris, a convert at Paul's hands, named in Acts 17:34 solely, but precisely, as an Athenian woman who believed when most others did not.

Lois and Eunice

Lois, her daughter Eunice, and Eunice's son Timothy were residents of the city of Lystra in Lycaonia. Apparently they were all converted by Paul and Barnabas on their journey together into Asia Minor. Timothy, whom Paul refers to in 1 Corinthians 4:17 as "my beloved and faithful child in the Lord," became one of Paul's most dependable helpers (see 1 Thess 3:2, 6; 1 Cor 4:17; 16:10; 2 Cor 1:19; Phil 2:19-24). His significance in Paul's missionary life is reflected in the later Deutero-Pauline tradition which addressed two of the Pastoral letters, 1 and 2 Timothy, to him. What is known about Timothy's grandmother and mother, Lois and Eunice, must be pieced together from brief statements in 2 Timothy and Acts.

The "Paul" writing 2 Timothy refers to Timothy's sincere faith, "a faith that dwelt first in your grandmother Lois and your mother Eunice" (1:5). A bit farther on, in respect to his religious upbringing, Timothy is reminded that "from childhood you have been acquainted with the sacred writings which are able to instruct you for salvation through faith in Christ Jesus" (3:15). The allusion could refer back to Lois and Eunice as Timothy's early teachers.

There is no reason to doubt the correctness of the author of this letter concerning the names of Timothy's mother and grandmother. It appears he was aware of a tradition that Timothy's conversion followed after Lois and Eunice had already become believers (2 Tim 1:5). But the idea that Timothy had been given an early introduction to the Scriptures, implying a rather orthodox upbringing, has been judged more a development of Christian legend[1] since it contradicts the tradition in Acts 16, which

---

[1]The author of 2 Timothy (see 1:3) is interested in the concept of a religious upbringing. 2 Timothy 3:15 serves as a development of that theme. See Martin Dibelius and Hans Conzelmann, *The Pastoral Epistles.* trans. by P. Buttolph and A. Yarbro from 4th German ed. 1966 (Philadelphia: Fortress, 1972) 98.

stresses that Timothy was uncircumcised—and therefore in reality the product of "a lax Judaism."[2]

Acts 16:1-3 refers to a period early in Paul's second journey when he arrives at Lystra and invites Timothy to accompany him. Timothy is described as "the son of a Jewish woman who was a believer; but his father was a Greek" (16:1). This text indicates that Timothy's mother Eunice was a Jewess who had married a Gentile and that later she had become Christian. (Although Acts makes no reference to Lois, evidently she was also Jewish.) The text also indicates that Timothy had never been circumcised, something Paul proceeded to do "because of the Jews that were in those places, for they all knew that his father was a Greek" (16:3).[3]

In the meager sketch of Eunice and Lois which these considerations suggest, what especially commands interest is the marital situation of Eunice and the question of whether her children were considered Jewish or Gentile. As a Jewess married to a Gentile, her union would undoubtedly have been disapproved from the Jewish perspective. It is common to find interpreters generalizing, however, that her offspring, as a result of their parents' intermarriage, would nevertheless be considered Jewish because they had a Jewish mother.

While rabbinic law does judge the offspring of intermarriage matrilineally, and while rabbinic texts seem to agree that the child of a Jewish woman by a Gentile man was a Jew, Shaye Cohen has recently reopened the case of Eunice and Timothy.[4] He questions whether the relevant rabbinic law (*m. Qidd.* 3:12) was already in existence in the first century C.E., and if so, whether the Jews of Asia Minor observed it. With respect to the first concern, Cohen finds that the matrilineal principle appears to originate only in the first quarter of the second century C.E. He also points out that even if it were of first century origin and existed in proto-rabbinic circles in Palestine, it cannot be assumed that it was known to and had been accepted by the Jews of Asia Minor.

[2]So Ernst Haenchen, *The Acts of the Apostles. A Commentary.* trans. by B. Noble and G. Shinn from 14th German ed. 1965 (Oxford: Blackwell, 1971) 478, n. 3.

[3]The non-interference of Timothy's father leads to the assumption he was dead. A few mss., e.g., 1838 gig, thus refer to Eunice as a widow in 16:1, but this reading is generally judged secondary.

[4]Shaye J. D. Cohen, "Was Timothy Jewish (Acts 16:1-3)? Patristic Exegesis, Rabbinic Law, and Matrilineal Descent," *Journal of Biblical Literature* 105 (1986) 251-268.

Cohen makes the interesting observation that, while scholars have usually held that from the time of Ezra the matrilineal principle was operative in Judaism, in fact certain biblical texts (e.g. Lev 24:10) make it clear that "lineage was matrilineal when it was matrilocal. When the Israelite woman moved abroad to join her Gentile husband, her children were considered Gentile."[5] For these reasons Cohen is quite decisive in stating that Timothy as a son of Eunice would not have been presumed to be Jewish by either Paul or the other Jews of Asia Minor.

Yet, Cohen's conclusion seems too tightly drawn, especially in respect to the very issue of matrilocality. It remains possible that the Diaspora Jewish community in a place such as Lystra, where Eunice lived, was sufficiently numerous or cohesive to consider her children by intermarriage as one of themselves. Furthermore, it has been argued that "the new attitudes which would lead to the eventually prevailing rabbinic opinion were already present"[6] among Eunice's compatriots. At the same time, Cohen's investigation serves well to warn against making a too facile assumption of what Eunice's children's status might have been among her people. Whatever it was, faith in Jesus brought change to their lives, first to Lois and Eunice, and eventually to Timothy.

In the end, it remains puzzling that Paul circumcised Timothy. Acts implies that were it not for the Jews Paul would not have done so (Acts 16:3). Did Paul circumcise him because in the eyes of Eunice's people her son was indeed a Jew who needed to be made fully acceptable to those Jews to whom he and Paul would minister? Or did Paul circumcise him because in the eyes of Eunice's family and friends her son was a Gentile and for that reason Paul was concerned that Jews might think Gentile Christians detested circumcision?[7] Full insight into Paul's motive eludes us, and likewise, unfortunately, so does Eunice's thought on the matter.

---

[5]*Ibid.*, 266.

[6]So Christopher Bryan, "A Further Look at Acts 16:1-3," *Journal of Biblical Literature* 107 (1988) 292–294, 294.

[7]For a full discussion, see Cohen, "Timothy," 251–263.

Damaris

To the northwest of the acropolis in Athens is a low hill known as the Areopagus, or Hill of Ares. This served as the original meeting place of an advisory council to the Athenian kings. Though the council's political power had declined over the centuries, it remained prestigious and continued to hold responsibility in matters of religion, morals, and homicide in the first century C.E. While the council derived its name from the hill meeting place, in Roman times it usually convened in the Royal Portico in the marketplace. Before this court Paul was invited to expound his teaching (cf. Acts 17:19, 22).[8] Acts 17:34 summarizes his partially successful preaching in this city by observing: "But some men joined him and believed, among them Dionysius the Areopagite and a woman named Damaris and others with them."

Who was Damaris, this Athenian believer? That her name is given implies some personal or social distinction. Was she one among the intellectuals who had listened to Paul speak to the Areopagus? Or someone who heard Paul in the synagogue or marketplace or tentmaking workshop (cf. 17:17)? The suggestions by various commentators that Damaris was the wife of Dionysius or the mother of one of the young philosophers of the Areopagus are unconvincing since the emphasis in the text, "and a woman named Damaris" (*kai gynē onomati Damaris*), is not on her marital or relational status but on her identity as a *female* convert.

It is of some interest to observe that this phrase, and thus all mention of Damaris, is omitted from the Western text manuscripts, most notably from Codex D. This is only one among a number of other variants in D which appear to either delete or diminish the mention or roles of women in some places where Luke gives them noticeable attention (e.g., Acts 1:14; 17:4, 12; 18:26). For this reason it has been charged that there is an anti-

---

[8]Cf. C. J. Hemer, "Paul at Athens: A Topographical Note," *New Testament Studies* 20 (1973–74) 344–350. Hemer thinks it most probable that Paul spoke near the Stoa. He observes that "the swift narrative [of Acts] tells against the assumption of delay or remand in prison while the court assembled on the hill. It is easier to think it was in session nearby. And the conversion of a woman [Damaris] and others unnamed . . . suggests further the characteristic crowd of interested spectators of a hearing which had become the *cause célèbre* of the moment, conducted in the relative publicity of the Agora" (350).

feminist tendency in D's (i.e., the Western) textual tradition.[9] In an assessment of this data, Ben Witherington writes:

> In view of the . . . evidence, it appears that there was a concerted effort by some part of the Church, perhaps as early as the late first century or beginning of the second, to tone down texts in Luke's second volume that indicated that women played an important and prominent part in the days of the Christian community. William Ramsay long ago remarked with some justification that in reaction to the conventions in various parts of the Roman Empire, "the Universal and Catholic type of Christianity became confirmed in its dislike of the prominence and public ministration of women. The dislike became abhorrence, and there is every probability that the dislike is as old as the first century, and was intensified to abhorrence before the middle of the second century." In fact, [Witherington responds], it seems more likely that the "Western" text was simply reflecting Roman and Western ideas about women not playing prominent roles in public life. In any event, the evidence

[9]The charge is not new. For reflections on it see Ben Witherington, "The Anti-Feminist Tendencies of the 'Western' Text in Acts," *Journal of Biblical Literature* 103 (1984) 82–84. Cf. Bruce Metzger, *A Textual Commentary on the Greek New Testament* (London: United Bible Society, 1971) 459, who holds that Codex D's omission of Damaris resulted inadvertently from scribal error in omitting one line of text.

Reference is made a few times throughout this study to readings found in the so-called Western text. This manuscript group includes a number of textual witnesses, the most important of which are the Old Latin manuscripts and Codex D (= Bezae). On the Western text see esp. Haenchen, *Acts,* 50–60. Most notably entering into our discussion is Codex D, which dates from the fifth or possibly sixth century and contains most of the four Gospels and Acts (and a fragment of 3 John). The text is presented in Greek and Latin, the two languages facing each other on opposite pages. It has been observed by Metzger that "no known manuscript has so many and such remarkable variations from what is usually taken to be the normal New Testament text. Codex Bezae's special characteristic is the free addition (and occasional omission) of words, sentences, and even incidents" (*The Text of the New Testament* (Oxford: Clarendon, 2nd. ed. 1968) 50.

Scholars have reflected extreme positions in regard to the Western text. Some have shown (and continue to do so) a one-sided preference for its readings; others have regarded it as totally corrupt. While neither extreme is currently given general support, the readings of these witnesses are normally taken seriously and given at least a hearing. See the remarks by Max Wilcox, "Luke and the Bezan Text of Acts," in Jacob Kremer, *Les Actes des Apôtres. Traditions, redaction, theologie.* BETL 48 (Leuven: University Press, 1979) 447–455. With respect to the additions, there is always a suspicion that they are inauthentic elaborations on the text, but it is also possible that the Western text might preserve original readings lost to other texts or in its additions reflect original traditions.

. . . is sufficient to bear witness that Luke's attempt to give women special prominence in Acts soon rubbed people the wrong way.[10]

Because Codex D's omission of Damaris has generally not been held to reflect the original text, she fortunately has remained known to readers of the New Testament, a small but nevertheless meaningful victory in the struggle for survival of the story of women in the early church.

But was Damaris actually one of Paul's converts? The statement by Paul in 1 Corinthians 16:15 that the household of Stephanas were "the first converts in Achaia," raises this issue. Ought not Damaris, Dionysius and the other Athenians to have been given that distinction? This has caused Ernst Haenchen to conclude that Luke might have known a report about a congregation which existed later in Athens, in which Damaris and Dionysius were mentioned, and interpreted it as referring to the period immediately following Paul's speech.[11] Yet it can also be supposed that Paul's Athenian missionizing was so overwhelmingly disappointing compared to his success shortly thereafter with the Corinthians, that it was Corinthian converts who stood out in his memory as his outstanding first converts in Achaia. Yet if such were the case, it appears Damaris and Dionysius were relegated to some obscurity even in Paul's thinking. Nevertheless, their names managed to survive in the traditions know to Luke, and Damaris herself has triumphed over the additional assault of the Western text.

To conclude, Eunice, Lois, and Damaris are women of whom the New Testament tells us very little, yet they captivate our curiosity. In examining just a few details about each we are drawn into their lives, wanting to understand their situations more fully even though there are so few fragments to put together. But a paucity of information does not prevent these three early Christians from offering us an important witness about some of the women who became members of Paul's communities: Eunice and

---

[10]Witherington, "Anti-Feminist Tendencies," 83–84. Ramsay is cited from his *St. Paul the Traveller and the Roman Citizen* (London: Hodder and Stoughton, 1st ed. 1895) 252.

[11]Haenchen, *Acts,* 526.

Lois, residents of a small city, remind us that there were Hellenistic Jewesses, some of whom were in mixed marriages[12] and thus difficult social situations. Damaris, in contrast, symbolizes Gentile women from large cities, women living in the midst of all that Greek culture and urban development had to offer.

To think of these very different people responding to Paul's preaching of the Lord is to raise the question of how Christianity could attract, absorb, and bond together these and so many other types of women. Ironically, the answer is probably not lost in all that we do not know about these people but stares at us in those very comments provided by the New Testament. The bond was obviously faith, and then—as now—belief in the Lord apparently moved mountains in helping each of these people to meld their lives into the Christian movement.

[12]A relevant study which appeared after this text was written is Margaret Y. Mac-Donald, "Early Christian Women Married to Unbelievers," *Studies in Religion/Sciences Religieuses* 19 (1990) 221-234.

3

Household Heads:
Lydia, Chloe, Nympha

Among Paul's female converts, friends, and acquaintances were several household heads such as Lydia, Chloe, and Nympha. In the case of Lydia and Nympha, it appears that they were likewise leaders of the Churches which met in their homes. As for Chloe, while members of her household seem to have been Christian, it is not certain that she herself belonged to the Church.

The assumption is normally made by New Testament interpreters that women who were household heads came into such an independent position as a result of being widowed, divorced, or never married. While that is generally a sound supposition to make, it is also known that under the *lex Iulia de maritandis ordinibus* (18 B.C.E.) and the *lex Papia Poppaea* (9 C.E.) freeborn women with three children and freed women with four (after manumission) were allowed a number of privileges, including the right to apply through an official for permission to make legal transactions without first obtaining the consent of their guardian or husband.[1] This right was commonly referred to as the *ius*

---

[1] See G.H.R. Horsley, *New Documents Illustrating Early Christianity. A Review of the Greek Inscriptions Published in 1976, 1977, 1978*, 3 vols. (North Ryde, N.S.W.: Ancient History Documentary Research Center, Macquarie University, 1981–83). The reference here is to *New Docs 1977*, 29–32.

liberorum. Various papyri from the Roman period witness to women who exercised it.[2] Therefore the usual conclusion that women like Lydia, Chloe, and Nympha were without husbands must be qualified with the possibility, albeit a minor one, that such women may have had husbands but nevertheless were accustomed to acting in the spirit of the *ius liberorum*. If so, they would have carried on their business dealings and their involvement with Paul and their Churches in a similar fashion.

Lydia

Lydia was a Philippian resident and, as far as can be known, Paul's first convert on European soil. The sum total of New Testament information about her is found in the Acts narrative which describes Paul founding the Church at Philippi (16:11-40):

> We [Paul, Silas and Luke] remained in this city [Philippi] some days; and on the sabbath day we went outside the gate to the riverside, where we supposed there was a place of prayer; and we sat down and spoke to the women who had come together. One who heard us was a woman named Lydia, from the city of Thyatira, a seller of purple goods, who was a worshipper of God. The Lord opened her heart to give heed to what was said by Paul. And when she was baptized with her household, she besought us, saying, "if you have judged me to be faithful to the Lord, come to my house and stay." And she prevailed upon us (16:13-15).

> [At the end of the Philippian visit, which had resulted in the imprisonment of Paul and Silas] . . . they went out of the prison, and visited Lydia; and when they had seen the brethren, they exhorted them[3] and departed (16:40).

It has always puzzled commentators, considering the significance Acts accords to Lydia, that Paul himself never mentions

---

[2]Portefaix, *Sisters*, p. 9, observes that it can be assumed that a wife in a good marriage would have had no real need to pursue this legal privilege.

[3]Codex D describes Paul and Silas as reporting the events at Lydia's house not merely to inform the congregation, but to provide edifying proof of what the Lord had done for them.

her in his only extant epistle to the Philippians.[4] This has fueled speculation that either Luke, or pious imagination before him, conjured up Lydia. Yet, because Acts' statements about her are embedded within a set of verses (16:11-15) which have the character of a travel narrative reflecting apparently accurate information (e.g. correct details are given about the status of the colony of Philippi and the smallness of the local Jewish community), it seems reasonable to assume the general historical reliability of the assertions about Lydia.[5] On the other hand, even if Lydia were to be judged not historical, she may well be representative of a type of Christian woman in the Pauline Churches as their traditions were known to the author of Acts and thus of much interest to our survey.

Lydia, originally from Thyatira, is said to have been a resident of Philippi, a worshipper of God and a seller of purple goods when she was converted to Christianity about 50 C.E. Because the city of Thyatira in the Roman province of Asia was in a district known as Lydia, it can be assumed that her name had been applied descriptively to her in Philippi, i.e., "the Lydian woman." This suggests that she once had servile status,[6] since slaves were often given a name reflecting their geographical origin. However, she must have achieved her freedom because she had her own household in Philippi. Furthermore, her occupation as a seller of purple goods is one known from various inscriptions to have been held in many instances by ex-slaves.[7] It has also been noted that Lydia's name is a Latinized form of the Greek *Lydē*. This could be a clue that her former owner was one of the Roman residents of Philippi,[8] a not implausible suggestion since that city was a Roman *colonia,* a place where Romans, especially veterans, were encouraged to settle.

---

[4]On the hypothesis that the mention of Euodia or Syntyche in Philippians in fact refers to Lydia, see below, p. 46. Regarding the theory that the puzzling reference to *gnēsie syzyge,* "Yokefellow," in Phil 4:3 also denotes Lydia, see also, p. 46.

[5]So the form critical analysis of vv. 11-15 by Haenchen, *Acts,* 502.

[6]See Horsley, *New Docs 1977,* 27.

[7]*Ibid.,* 27. According to Sarah B. Pomeroy, *Goddesses, Whores, Wives and Slaves: Women in Classical Antiquity* (New York: Schocken, 1975) 200, freedwomen from the eastern provinces often traded in luxury goods such as purple dye or perfumes.

[8]So Horsley, *New Docs 1977,* 27-28.

Little can be said about Lydia's origins or her earlier life in
Thyatira. It may be suggested that her knowledge of the purple
goods business began there since Thyatira is known to have had
prosperous dyers among its prominent trade guilds. It cannot be
determined when Lydia left Thyatira nor whether she was already
a "worshipper of God" before arriving in Philippi.

Lydia met Paul during his first visit to Philippi when he and
his companions had gone outside the gate on the sabbath to the
riverbanks supposing to find there a place of prayer, a *proseuchē.*
Paul encountered a group gathered to pray, all of them women,
to whom he then preached. Lydia was converted on that occasion and subsequently baptized along with her household.

Apparently the Jews of the area and their proselytes met on
the riverbank either in the absence of a synagogue in Philippi or
because the practice of their religion, although licit in the Romans'
view, was forbidden inside that particular city.[9] Whatever the reason for the prayer spot, its location as that significant place where
"the Lord opened Lydia's heart" (16:14) has been difficult for
archaeologists to determine.[10] In the nineteenth century the remains of a Roman archway could still be seen in the ruins of
Philippi on the west side of the city, although that has now disappeared completely. The archway dated from the approximate
time of Paul and was probably built when Philippi became a
Roman colony (ca. 42 B.C.E.) to symbolize the dignity and
privileges which the city enjoyed. It may also have marked the
line of the *pomerium,* the demarcation inside of which foreign
cults and burials were not allowed. The route of the *Via Egnatia*
as it left Philippi to the west went beneath this arch and then,
about a mile and a half from the city, it crossed the Ganga or
Gangites River.

Some have thought that this colonial arch must be the gate mentioned in 16:13, and it was thus the Gangites that had served as
Lydia's fateful meeting place with Paul. However, since the arch

[9]Cf. Acts 16:20-21 for a reflection of Philippian hostility to Jews. See also Thomas
Derek, "The Place of Women in the Church at Philippi," *Expository Times* 83 (1972)
117-120, 117. Portefaix, *Sisters,* 73, reports that there are no archaeological traces
of Judaism within the colony nor are there remains of any synagogue.

[10]See Jack Finegan, *The Archaeology of the New Testament: The Mediterranean
World of the Early Christian Apostles* (Boulder, Colo.: Westview Press, 1981) 103-104;
Meeks, *Urban Christians,* 211, n. 237.

was more than a mile outside the city, the question is raised whether the women would have gone so far to pray. It has been proposed, alternatively, that the gate in 16:13 was more likely the Krenides Gate, located in the western wall of the city, a gate which has also been located and excavated. In that case, the river prayer place would have been on the Krenides Stream, very near the edge of the city. Locally that place is now known as the River of Lydia.

However, there is one more location in Philippi suggested as the place where Paul and Lydia met, a spot on the eastern side of the city outside the Neapolis Gate where a small stream flows. A Christian basilica dating from the first half of the fourth century has been excavated there. The relatively early date for the construction of a church on that spot, puzzlingly outside the walls, could be explained if the site had been remembered as the area of Paul's early ministry and Lydia's baptism. Interestingly, no evidence of a baptistery has been found, perhaps suggesting that baptism even in the era of the basilica was still done in the running stream where Paul presumably had first encountered and then baptized Lydia and his other Philippian converts.

While there are no details in Acts about Lydia's baptism, it very likely took place by immersion. On the basis of that assumption it has been speculated that because Paul and his male companions would hardly have presided at the immersion of a woman, they must have had one or more female co-workers with them.[11] But this inference is not convincing for it seems to presume that Paul's ministry was totally separated from (as later Christianity would be) the Jewish milieu. But, for Jewish women and proselytes, as well as for Jewish males like Paul, proselyte baptism and ritual immersion (e.g., the *miqveh*) were common, familiar practices. Certainly the Jewish women of Philippi could have conducted the immersion aspect of Lydia's baptism for her and the others among themselves who desired baptism without the aid of an outsider female co-worker of Paul. The immersion baptism of initial female converts like Lydia thus suggests not so much that Paul had to have female co-workers in his company when he founded Churches,[12] as it does that ministry to the initial converts of a

[11]See Ellen Juhl Christiansen, "Women and Baptism," *Studia Theologica* 35 (1981) 1–8, 3.

[12]Undoubtedly there were times when Paul did have female co-workers, e.g., Prisca in Corinth and Ephesus.

Church derived not only from an outside missionary like Paul coming in, but must have come immediately also from among the converts themselves.[13]

As a seller of purple goods, a *porphyropolis,* Lydia was involved in an occupation which required some capital.[14] Her goods would have been purple dye and purple-dyed articles, pieces of fabric, perhaps imported to Philippi from Thyatira or maybe from nearby Thessalonica where there is also known to have been a purple dyeing industry.[15] Lydia's trade has been described as one "entirely connected to the feminine sphere"[16] since purple was used in the household for the dyeing of fabrics, especially for festive dresses and also as a rouge for cheeks and lips. Therefore, "a woman dealer in purple needed to be well dressed herself in order to advertise her goods as her appearance would place her high in the estimation of other women."[17]

The most valued color-fast purple dye was obtained from the Tyrian murex, a mollusk found along the Syrian and Phoenician coasts. The people of that area had a monopoly on the dye through much of ancient history. But in the early Christian period, as inscriptional evidence reveals, there was imperial control over the purple dye-works in Tyre.[18] And, an inscription in Miletus indicates that that Roman administration went back at least to

[13]By way of trajectory, it is interesting to note that Lydia and the other women in Philippi who participated in the early Christian community in that city form the remote backdrop for some conclusions drawn by Valerie Abrahamsen, "Christianity and the Rock Reliefs at Philippi," *Biblical Archaeologist* 51 (1988) 46–56. Abrahamsen observes that several generations after Paul had evangelized the city, when theoretically Christianity should have been well established and flourishing, numerous depictions of gods and particularly goddesses were carved into an acropolis hill which she judges were created and used primarily by women, notably the socially powerless women of Philippi. On the basis of these carvings, this author theorizes that the daughters and later descendants of Lydia's generation of Pauline converts became syncretistic in their Christian praxis with the result that Christianity became not only a minor religious force in Philippi between 150–300 C.E. (after which it is known to have been dominant) but also was "of a rather different sort in that period than the Church fathers were promulgating" (54).

[14]On the purple dyeing industry and Lydia, see Rosalie Ryan, "Lydia, A Dealer in Purple Goods," *The Bible Today* 2 (1984) 285–289.

[15]See Meeks, *Urban Christians,* 46.

[16]Portefaix, *Sisters,* 170.

[17]*Ibid.,* 171.

[18]See Horsley, *New Docs 1977,* 25–27.

the period of Nero (54–68 C.E.). G.H.R. Horsley has suggested that those involved in the imperially controlled purple trade— whose names reflect that they were primarily of freed status— were thus members of the *familia Caesaris,* i.e., the emperor's civil service throughout the empire. He further speculates that if the imperial monopoly were initiated prior to Nero, perhaps by Claudius (41–54 C.E.), since he is often claimed to have been a great innovator in centralized administration, then we might be led to identify Lydia more exactly as a member of "Caesar's household."[19] Horsley suggests this about Lydia as being no more than an intriguing possibility. Further support to be added to his suggestion, however, is the reference in Philippians 4:22 to those in Caesar's service who send their greetings to the Philippians. Could it be that those greetings were actually from, among others, Lydia who had either moved away from Philippi or was on business in the area where the imprisoned Paul wrote Philippians?[20] Might this not also explain why Lydia herself is not greeted in the letter?

Were Lydia indeed a member of the *familia Caesaris,* this would open up new avenues of investigation into her life as a freed woman selling purple in the first century C.E.[21] Yet, much hesitation remains in pursuing that possibility since the theory of her belonging to the *familia* is based on the assumption that Lydia dealt with goods colored with the expensive Tyrian purple. A less expensive dye obtained from the roots of the madder plant, the so-called "Turkey red," was also in use at the time, notably in western Asia Minor, and there is no evidence it was under any form of imperial control.[22] If the latter were the type of dye Lydia dealt in, and there is no way to be certain, then her trade would have been separate from the royal monopoly, and there would be no reason to suppose she was a freedwoman of the imperial household.

[19]*Ibid.,* 28.

[20]Theories on the location of this imprisonment variously place it in Ephesus, Rome, or Caesarea.

[21]On the *familia Caesaris,* see especially P.R.C. Weaver, *Familia Caesaris. A Social Study of the Emperor's Freedmen and Slaves* (Cambridge: Cambridge University Press, 1972).

[22]See Horsley, *New Docs 1978,* 53–54.

Lydia's status as a "worshipper of God" (*sebomenē ton theon,* i.e., a god-fearer), is another aspect of her identity which has also drawn attention in recent scholarship. The very existence of a group of Gentiles known as god-fearers and considered to be partial converts to Judaism, long accepted by New Testament scholars, has been called into question primarily by A. Thomas Kraabel. Kraabel took the position that god-fearers function merely as a Lukan device to show how Christianity moved from its proclamation within Judaism to become a Gentile religion.[23]

If Kraabel is right, then in the case of Lydia, for example, we would be more inclined to suspect that not just her religious status but her very existence is due to Luke's imagination. In fact, however, Kraabel's revisionist position has been widely challenged as overstated. A number of studies, including Louis Feldman's analysis of various god-fearer inscriptions and literary references,[24] appear to have tipped the balance back to the probable existence of such a group of people. And Kraabel himself has conceded that god-fearers actually existed but what he really contested was "the size and cohesiveness of the godfearers; there were not millions of them as sometimes claimed, and they did not form a distinct social class."[25]

More than a reaffirmation of the existence of the god-fearers, however, has resulted from the debate sparked by Kraabel. The extensive examination of the evidence about them has led to reminders about arriving at premature conclusions. A case in point, as Feldman has made clear, is that in the first century C.E. those called god-fearers (various terms were used apparently without technical distinction: "those fearing," *phoboumenoi*; "those reverencing God," *sebomenoi ton theon*; "God worshippers," *theosebeis*; and "those who fear," *meteuntes,* were *not* limited to semi-proselytes but can also be found referring at least

---

[23]See A. Thomas Kraabel, "The Disappearance of the 'God-Fearers,'" *Numen* 28 (1981) 113–126.

[24]Louis H. Feldman, "The Omnipresence of the God-Fearers," *Biblical Archaeology Review* 12 (no. 5, 1986) 58–69.

[25]Kraabel made this concession at the 1986 annual meeting of the Society of Biblical Literature as recorded in a report of the meeting in *Biblical Archaeology Review* 13 (no. 2, 1987) 52.

in one instance to full converts (cf. Acts 13:43: "devout converts," *sebomenoi prosēlytoi*).[26]

As far as Lydia is concerned, this opens the question of her precise status. Was Luke portraying her as a semi-proselyte as has usually been assumed, or was she a full convert? While Lydia was obviously sabbath observant and would have had no obstacle (such as male circumcision) to prevent her full conversion, there is not enough evidence to determine exactly where she stood.

An additional slant on Lydia as a god-fearer has also entered into interpretative discussions, this from the perspective of sociological analysis. Abraham Malherbe has pointed out that Luke's account of Lydia's conversion shows that not only the theological implications of that conversion were important to him, but also the sociological.[27] Malherbe asserts that Jews had an ambivalent attitude toward proselytes and god-fearers, and that even despite the degrees to which these people adopted Judaism, social inequality between them and the Jews seemed to be an ongoing fact of life. Thus, with Lydia's challenging invitation to Paul, "If you have judged me to be faithful to the Lord, come to my house and stay" (Acts 16:15), Malherbe thinks Luke is making the claim that such social inequality ought not to exist within the Church.

If Malherbe's interpretation is correct, as well it might be, the question arises whether Lydia herself, and not just Luke, would have been responsible for addressing the challenge to Paul to resist perpetuating social inequality among the Christians. Would this woman have protested her own hitherto socially unfair treatment? Although any answer is but a mere guess, given the overall independent nature with which Acts describes Lydia, the person whom Luke envisioned was undoubtedly capable of raising the issue.[28]

---

[26]Feldman, "Omnipresence," 59.

[27]Abraham Malherbe, *Social Aspects of Early Christianity* (Baton Rouge: Louisiana State University Press, 1977) 66–67.

[28]A different, although not uncomplementary, interpretation of Lydia's invitation is that offered from the French structuralist perspective by Yann Redalié, "Conversion or Liberation? Notes on Acts 16:11-40" in *The Bible and Liberation. Political and Social Hermeneutics. A Radical Religion Reader* coordinated by N. K. Gottwald and A. C. Wire (Berkeley: The Community for Religous Research and Education, 1976) 102–108. Redalié, who views the river place of prayer as "the Jewish space," sees Lydia's request as making possible "leaving the Jewish space and opening up a new place" (104).

One suspects that a woman such as Lydia must have viewed Paul from a rather detached, independent perspective. Because her world had broad horizons, and given her socio-economic status, in a sense she needed nothing from him. Already financially established through her household and her business, she had apparently also known both upward social mobility in her transition from slavery to freed status and the spiritual satisfaction of attaching herself to the God of the Jewish people. On the other hand, Lydia may also have felt a disappointing sense of social discrimination at the hands of those very chosen people with whom she had cast her lot. When Paul's preaching touched her heart, Lydia's sincere response might therefore have been tempered with a wariness about the preacher. Would this person who urged Lydia to be baptized identify himself socially with her and her household? Would he who preached the unity of believers in the Lord put himself where his words were? If such questions were in Lydia's mind, perhaps she was actually surprised when Paul and his companions accepted her invitation of hospitality. Lydia must have rejoiced not only at hearing the good news of the Lord but in experiencing the sincerity of the messenger.

Chloe

Chloe is referred to by Paul in 1 Corinthians 1:11 because her "people," literally *hoi tōn Chloēs,* "those of Chloe," had informed Paul about quarreling among the Corinthians. Chloe's people must have been either family members or slave or freed employees of her household. The report Paul received from them while he was in Ephesus could have been conveyed either by letter or word of mouth. However, it is not evident where these people were from. Since the Corinthians apparently knew Chloe, she and her household may well have lived among them. But an Ephesian rather than a Corinthian residence seems more probable since Paul would hardly have been so tactless as to identify his informants in 1 Corinthians 1:11 in remarks to their local brothers and sisters.

To have run a business which necessitated sending representatives to Corinth suggests Chloe was a person of some capital. But while she was obviously rather well off, it is not clear if she had become a Christian, although her people were evidently so. It has been pointed out, however, that the description of her emissaries as *hoi tōn Chloēs* contrasts with phrases referring to Christian members of other households, e.g., *hoi ek tōn Aristoboulou, hoi ek tōn Narkissou* (Rom 16:10-11). The omission of the preposition *ek*, "from," in the phrase mentioning Chloe could imply that the whole of her household including Chloe herself was Christian.[29] It might also be that Paul's identification of his informants by using Chloe's name reflects his actual acquaintance with her, perhaps through business, but just as likely through membership in the Christian community. Chloe, like Lydia, may well have been known to Paul as a woman who believed along with her whole household.

If indeed Chloe was Christian, which still remains an open question, she and Lydia together would suggest a type of woman who belonged to the Pauline Churches: female heads of households and businesses, women thus accustomed to leadership and decision-making roles. Another such person was Nympha.

Nympha

Nympha and "the church in her house" are greeted by "Paul" at the end of Colossians (4:15). Many infer from the text that Nympha lived in Laodicea, although the ambiguity of the Colossian reference to her has allowed commentators to conclude that her home and the group she hosted may also have been in either Colossae or Hierapolis. From Colossians 4:15 it can be assumed that Nympha was a household head, perhaps also a more independently acting married woman, and host to the Christians who met in her house. Presumably Nympha was the leader of that house church.

There is some discussion among scholars concerning whether Paul always viewed house churches as parts of local churches or whether house church and local church might not be synonymous terms in some Pauline contexts.[30] In the case of Nympha, Marlis Gielen, for example, holds that Nympha's house church is a local (thus not a partial) church. Gielen reaches this conclusion by see-

[29]So Meeks, *Urban Christians*, 217, n. 54.

[30]See e.g., Marlis Gielen, "Zur Interpretation der paulinischen Formel *hē kat' oikon ekklēsia*," *Zeitschrift für die neutestamentliche Wissenschaft* 77 (1986) 109–125.

ing an analogy between the reference to the Laodiceans in Colossians 4:15 which indicates a local church and the immediately following greetings to Nympha's group which this scholar argues must be the local church of Hierapolis since that group is not greeted elsewhere in the letter.[31] This reasonable deduction that Nympha's group was the local church at Hierapolis suggests that we should view her not as the head of one group among many such Christian cells in one city, but as the leader of the entire Church in Hierapolis.

How Nympha and Paul became acquainted remains unclear, although like all those Paul is portrayed as having known in Colossae, Laodicea, and Hierapolis,[32] places he is never known to have visited, one supposes his initial contacts with these people took place in Ephesus during his long stay there in the mid 50s. If that were the case with Nympha, it might be surmised that for her as a household head to have travelled to Ephesus indicates she may have been on business travel and was thus in a social position similar to that of Lydia and Chloe.

The memory of Nympha has survived in the New Testament but not without a battle. Her gender, taken to be feminine for example by the RSV, has been the subject of scrutiny since her name in Greek is written in the accusative case, *Nymphan*. This form could refer to a female named Nympha or to a male named Nymphas. The question has been complicated by manuscript variations in the possessive pronoun modifying "house" in Colossians 4:15. Some ancient texts read *autēs*, "her," others *autou*, "his," and yet others, *autōn*, "their." The feminine reading is the most difficult to explain and thus more likely to be the original. The masculine form can be explained as a correction of the feminine name by copyists who considered it either impossible or undesirable that a woman should have a leadership role. The reading with "their" likely arose when scribes included in the pronoun an earlier mention of *adelphous*, "brethren," in Colossians 4:15.

[31]*Ibid.*, 123–124.

[32]Where there is the possibility (as with Colossians) or probability (as with 2 Thessalonians, Ephesians, 1-2 Timothy and Titus) of Deutero-Pauline authorship, our approach is that persons who are mentioned only in these letters are not assumed to be necessarily fictitious but taken to have some historical basis in traditions known to the Deutero-Pauline authors.

Nympha serves as a stark reminder that not only is little told about women in the New Testament, but for some of the few who are mentioned there have been struggles just to keep their very names and gender in the text. But a battle with commentators' preconceived notions concerning the roles women may have had in their lives also has raged. Even those who acknowledge the high probability that *Nymphan* refers to a woman and that *autēs,* "her," evidently must be the original pronoun, nevertheless can still be predisposed to deny Nympha even the possibility of a leadership role in her housechurch. For example, J. L. Houlden has commented that if the text refers to a woman "then she was probably the most affluent of the congregation at Laodicea, or possibly Hierapolis, who was able most easily to let her house be used for meetings of the Church."[33] But should the text refer to a man, which Houlden admits is less probable, "then we are likely to have a reference to the leader (we cannot tell what his title will have been: elder, overseer/bishop?) of the church there, as well as its host."[34]

In striking contrast to this assessment stands one by Robert Banks:

> If, as seems most natural, Nympha was a relatively wealthy woman who, like Gaius at Corinth, acted as host to a local group of believers, it seems unlikely that she, presumably a widow who conducted her family, managed her slaves and welcomed her friends all week, would take an insignificant part in the proceedings in favor of socially inferior male members who were present. To do that would be socially unacceptable whereas, in the absence of a husband, it would be perfectly legitimate in the eyes of others for her to behave in home and church *as her husband would have done* if present. Most probably male heads of other households also belonged to this church and had an influential role in its activities but, given her position, Nympha would have functioned alongside them in similar sorts of ways, not in a subordinate capacity.[35]

[33]J. L. Houlden, *Paul's Letters From Prison: Philippians, Colossians, Philemon and Ephesians.* Westminster Pelican Commentaries (Philadelphia: Westminister, 1970) 221.

[34]*Ibid.*

[35]Robert Banks, *Paul's Idea of Community. The Early House Churches in Their Historical Setting* (Grand Rapids: Eerdmans, 1980) 127. Italics are his.

The lives of Lydia, Chloe, and Nympha when viewed together as household heads and, in the case of Lydia and Nympha as house church leaders,[36] perhaps also with Chloe if she was a Christian, hint at a pattern about one type of woman who joined the Pauline Churches. These three represent rather independent-minded, economically well-established women who seemingly felt an affinity with communities founded by Paul. This suggests that their becoming Christian had in no way placed them in an uncomfortable situation. There is no indication that as Christians they had radically altered their personalities or their ways of acting. It must be assumed therefore that as participants in their Christian groups they continued to function as "themselves," active and decisive leaders within their own spheres of concern. This pattern outlined here also implies that, correspondingly, Paul was unthreatened by this type of woman. His leadership was evidently not premised on their diminution. This analysis, of course, is not startlingly new, but rather concurs with the general impression current scholarship reflects about Paul who in living out his own call and mission also appreciated, and depended upon, the roles, tasks, and gifts of all the members of his communities. The presence in Christian groups of Lydia and Nympha, perhaps Chloe too, and the women these three typify was clearly welcomed by Paul. In contrast, he and they stand as a challenge (and a question concerning continuity with the New Testament Churches) to those modern Christian groups where active, decisive leadership-type women are discouraged or even prohibited from being themselves due to the prejudices, fears, or insecurities of others.

---

[36]Prisca also held this role. See below, pp. 52–53.

4

Co-Workers with the Apostle:
Euodia and Syntyche, Prisca

Three of the women who knew Paul and with whom he labored in the gospel, Euodia, Syntyche, and Prisca, are specifically referred to by Paul as his *synergoi,* "fellow-workers" (Phil 4:3; Rom 16:3). Paul accords this title not only to these three but also to various men.[1] It is one of the most frequently found of the designations Paul used to speak of his many associates.[2] Briefly defined, according to a significant study by Wolf-Henning Ollrog, a co-worker is "one who works together with Paul as an agent of God in the common work of missionary preaching."[3] Ollrog stresses at the same time that Paul also viewed himself as a co-worker, a self-perception rooted in his early work in the church at Antioch.[4]

[1]A complete list of all explicitly called *synergoi* includes Timothy (1 Thess 3:2; Rom 16:21); Apollos (1 Cor 3:9); Philemon (Phlm 1); Aristarchus, Mark, Demas, Luke, and probably Jesus Justus (Phlm 23-24; cf. Col 4:10-14); Epaphroditus (Phil 2:25); Euodia, Syntyche, Clement and others (Phil 4:2-3); Titus (2 Cor 8:23); Prisca and Aquila (Rom 16:3); Urbanus (Rom 16:9); indirectly Stephanas, Fortunatus, Achaicus, and others (1 Cor 16:15-18). Of course, the subject of Paul's co-workers involves more than those listed here since individuals such as Lydia or Nympha who are not given titles clearly also functioned as Paul's associates.

[2]Other often used terms are *adelphos,* "brother," *diakonos,* "deacon," *apostolos,* "apostle." On all of the terms used for the Pauline co-workers, see E. Earle Ellis, "Paul and His Co-Workers," *New Testament Studies* 17 (1970-71) 437-452.

[3]Wolf-Henning Ollrog, *Paulus und seine Mitarbeiter: Untersuchungen zu Theorie und Praxis der paulinischen Mission.* WMANT 50, Neukirchen-Vluyn: Neukirchener, 1979, 67.

[4]*Ibid.,* 13.

43

Among the conclusions about co-workers arrived at in Ollrog's study are the following four points:[5] Co-workers were (1) basically rooted in the communities which sent them on their mission as community delegates. (2) They were integrally related to Paul's mission historically (the breadth, depth, and success of the mission related to the use of co-workers) and theologically (Paul's use of co-workers gave his mission the character of being a shared function of the Church). (3) Paul's treatment of his co-workers as partners was based in the gospel and gave him no claim to dominating authority, i.e., there was no hierarchy directing the co-workers. (4) The relation of the co-workers to their communities remained essential to them. Thus, in Ollrog's view the circle of Paul's co-workers never took on an institutional character, nor was there any question of a school or a succession; co-workers came to Paul, worked with him for a limited time, then returned to their communities.

Ollrog's study divides Paul's co-workers into three groups:[6] (1) the inner circle of people, like Barnabas, Silvanus, and Timothy who worked with Paul over a long period of time and from place to place; (2) those individuals from Paul's Christian foundations who worked with Paul in their communities, e.g., Euodia and Syntyche; (3) independent missionaries whom Paul considered to be co-workers. This third type does not actually constitute a group given the individual activity of these people. Prisca belongs in this category.

Ollrog's tri-partite categorizing of the co-workers is helpful in trying to recognize patterns among the amorphous group of people to whom Paul gave this designation. His four major conclusions, however, as they have been evaluated by others have not received acceptance as a whole, the first and the fourth being judged not convincing.[7] It has been pointed out that there is in fact very little information about Churches sending workers to Paul's mission. Furthermore, it is quite possible even if such co-workers were originally delegates, as Ollrog purports, that they went on to become independent co-workers. In the last analysis, then, we really

[5]*Ibid.*, 234–235.

[6]*Ibid.*, 107–108.

[7]See e.g., Meeks, *Urban Christians,* 233, n. 65 and 234, n. 73. See also the review of Ollrog's book by Fred O. Francis in *Journal of Biblical Literature* 100 (1981) 660–662.

cannot be certain how important individual communities were in the sending, tenure, and return of Paul's co-workers.

Euodia, Syntyche, and Prisca as individuals within this broad category of Pauline co-workers offer us a glimpse of three women who shared their labors with Paul. From them we can try to gain insight into the types of women they are suggestive of who collaborated closely with Paul.

Euodia and Syntyche

Euodia and Syntyche were Christians at Philippi whom Paul describes as having "labored side by side" with him in the gospel along with Clement and other co-workers (Phil 4:2-3). The two women are mentioned in Philippians because of a disagreement they had. This came to Paul's attention probably via Epaphroditus (cf. 2:25).

The actual identity of Euodia and Syntyche, whose names are clearly feminine, Greek names also found in numerous places outside the New Testament, has been questioned on a few accounts. For example, while Syntyche is indisputably a woman's name as it appears in the Greek text of Philippians, it was asserted by Theodore of Mopsuestia that this person was really a male. Theodore claimed to have heard it said that Syntyche ought to have been spelled as the masculine Syntyches, and that "he" was in fact the jailer at Philippi (cf. Acts 16) and Euodia's husband. No substantiation exists for this idea, however, and there is also no textual evidence to support it.[8] Furthermore, the feminine plural pronouns *autais* and *haitines* in 4:3, which can only refer back to Euodia and Syntyche, require that both names be feminine.

Another identity theory, one advanced by the Tübingen school, assumed that Euodia and Syntyche were not individuals but symbols for Jewish and Gentile Christians respectively. This approach interpreted the person called "true yokefellow" in 4:3 as "the unifier," and held him to be Peter, seen from the perspective of his role as mediator between these two factions within the Church. But this elaborate interpretation assumes that Paul was prone to

---

[8]See G. F. Hawthorne, *Philippians.* Word Biblical Commentaries 43 (Waco: Word Books, 1983) 178-181.

writing with extremely obscure symbolism, hardly the usual Paul as he is known from his extant letters.

It has also been suggested that either Euodia or Syntyche was in fact the Lydia of Acts 16, her name there being an adjective indicating her place of origin, i.e., "the Lydian."[9] The important role played by Lydia in the founding of the Church at Philippi and the mystifying absence of any mention of her in Philippians has lent a bit of support to this otherwise merely conjectural hypothesis.

The quarrel between Euodia and Syntyche which occasioned Paul's reference to them must have affected the entire Philippian community or it would hardly have been brought up in correspondence to be read in the presence of the entire Church. Paul's concern for these women is thus indicative of their importance within the group, assumably because they were leaders, perhaps deacons[10] or heads of house churches. And, while the content of Euodia's and Syntyche's quarrel is never specified in Philippians, one wonders whether it was not related to matters of Church leadership. Whatever the case, Paul urges the two to be reconciled in the Lord, emphatically repeating the plea to each "I entreat [you]," *parakalō* (4:2). Paul asks them to be of one mind in Christ. And, to help bring that about, he urges a person referred to simply as "true yokefellow," *gnēsie syzyge,* to intervene. To this latter person (whose identity continues to stump commentators), Paul remarks that Euodia and Syntyche "labored side by side," *sunēthlēsan,* on behalf of the gospel with him, Clement, and his other fellow workers.

It has been asserted by F. X. Malinowski that *sunathlein,* which Paul uses elsewhere only in Philippians 1:27, where Malinowski holds that it implies resisting *external* opposition, must bear the same nuance in 4:3; i.e., it "suggests strife, danger, opposition, courage, memorable loyalty, not leadership, ministry, preaching, presiding."[11] This observation is then used by the same author to argue that Euodia and Syntyche could not have had leadership roles among the Philippian Christians since their activity was

---

[9]See above, p. 31.

[10]So Portefaix, *Sisters,* 138, n. 13.

[11]F. X. Malinowski, "The Brave Women of Philippi," *Biblical Theology Bulletin* 15 (1985) 60–64, 62.

outwardly oriented. But Malinowski overlooks the noticeable singling out of these women for mention along with Clement, which clearly underscores their distinct importance among the Philippians. Further, his theory ignores the probability that Euodia's and Syntyche's "laboring side by side," if indeed it be restricted to facing external opposition, which is debatable in both Philippians 1:27 and 4:3, was most likely carried on precisely in their role of being strong leaders or teachers. Hence the seriousness of their quarrel for the Church of Philippi. Finally, even if *sunathlein* did indicate that Euodia's and Syntyche's labor was only externally directed, one would also have to apply the same restriction to Paul, Clement, and the others whose work is included in the same verb. But such a restriction, particularly when applied to Paul's work, would obviously be contrived.

Paul himself, by reminding the mediator "true yokefellow" of Euodia's and Syntyche's collaboration with him, indicates respect for their work among the Philippians; in Paul's view the two women are clearly not to be degraded for their disagreement, but are to be recognized as valued members of his team.[12] There appears to be no reason to assume therefore, as some have proposed in the past,[13] that the two labored for the spread of the gospel only among the women in Philippi; nor should their dispute, and thus most subtly their work, be jokingly belittled as mere bickering in the Rosary Society. Rather, as the text implies, Euodia and Syntyche must be recognized as workers equal in importance and role to Clement and Paul's other co-workers.

A significant study by Lilian Portefaix which analyzes how first-century Philippian women would have received (that is understood and interpreted) Paul's letter to their Church offers us some information which might be suggestive of the way women like Euodia and Syntyche would have thought. As first generation Christians in Philippi, and presumably as Gentiles (given their names),[14] these women would have come into Christianity (even if they were god-fearers like Lydia, the first convert in their

---

[12]Hawthorne, *Philippians,* 180.

[13]See the summary in *ibid.,* 180.

[14]See Portefaix, *Sisters,* 137. n. 11, where she observes that the Gentile names of Euodia and Syntyche "are not to be found in the epigraphical material in Philippi, but these names turn up in inscriptions in other places."

Church), with primarily a pagan religious background. Portefaix's study concludes that in Philippi there were three deities who most notably attracted female worshippers: Diana, Dionysus, and Isis.[15] She maintains that consequently, due to the probable diversity of their pagan religious experience, it may be assumed that controversies existed among Philippian Christian women regarding their interpretation of the gospel message.[16] Perhaps the dispute of Euodia and Syntyche carried such overtones. But Portefaix also cites as another almost certain cause of disagreement among the Christian women the likelihood that the members were asked to disseminate the gospel on two levels, i.e., by supporting Paul financially (cf. Phil 4:14-16) and by spreading the message to families and friends by exemplifying it (cf. Phil 2:2-5; 4:5).

A married woman's position in Philippi (as elsewhere in the Greco-Roman world among pagans) regarding religious matters relating to the domestic cults observed at home placed her in a role of subordination to her husband as the high priest of the family. Thus Portefaix sees little opportunity for Christian wives in mixed marriages to make personal contributions to the spread of the Church. In turn, this could have resulted in the need for women who were part of fully Christian families to carry a heavier burden in that work. This, then, could have caused hard feelings on their part. While Euodia's and Syntyche's quarrel may have been along these lines, as noted above, their disagreement could also very well have been over matters related to their being Church leaders. In any case, Portefaix's portrayal of Philippian women broadens our perception of the possible issues which may have been of concern to them.

In the end, we will probably never know why Euodia and Syntyche quarreled nor why it was of such concern to Paul. What matters, however, is their obvious importance to Paul and his great esteem for them. This is reflected in his statement that these two women, along with Clement and his other fellow workers are named "in the book of life" (4:3). Probably Paul drew this image from the figurative language of the Hebrew Bible where it refers to the great register of the covenantal people of God, the list of the righteous (Exod 32:32; Pss 69:28; 139:16). As Paul applies

[15]See *ibid.*, 75-128.
[16]See *ibid.*, 137-138.

it to Euodia and Syntyche, it is an indication of the profound respect which he felt they deserved.

Prisca

Prisca, as she is known in Paul's letters (or Priscilla, the diminutive form by which she is referred to in Acts), was one of the most cosmopolitan and well-travelled women mentioned in the New Testament traditions (see Acts 18:2, 18, 26; Rom 16:3; 1 Cor 16:19; 2 Tim 4:19).[17] She was married to Aquila, a Jew from Pontus whose trade was tentmaking. Together they were prominent in Christian missionary activity and friends of Paul over a period of many years. Their story, at least as Christians, begins in Rome.

It is not known why Aquila left his native Pontus in Bithynia, nor where he travelled and lived on his way to Rome (perhaps Jerusalem? cf. Acts 2:19). It is also uncertain where Prisca came from and where they were married. Her Latin name could indicate that she was a Roman, although Aquila's name was also Latin and both might reflect merely the custom of Greeks and Jews to take on such names while living in Rome.

In respect to Prisca's origin, some speculation has been given to a possible connection between her name and the *Coemeterium Priscillae,* one of the oldest catacombs in Rome. That cemetery seems to have originated as the burial place of Acilius Glabrio and other members of the Acilian family. Acilius Glabrio, consul with Trajan in 91 C.E., was put to death four years later under Domitian on a charge of practicing Judaism and atheism, which from the perspective of the Romans could have meant he was a Christian.[18] This might imply that Christianity had penetrated the *gens Acilia,* a leading Roman family, rather early. Since one of the names borne by the Acilian females was Priscilla or Prisca, the question arises whether the Prisca of the New Testament was

---

[17]On Prisca see especially Fiorenza, "Missionaries," 428–431; Bruce, *Pauline Circle,* 44–50; Ollrog, *Mitarbeiter,* 24–27; Luise Schottroff, "Women as Followers of Jesus in New Testament Times: An Exercise in Social-Historical Exegesis," in Norman K. Gottwald (ed.), *The Bible and Liberation, Political and Social Hermeneutics* (New York: Orbis, 1983) 418–427, 424–427.

[18]See Suetonius, *The Lives of the Twelve Caesars: Domitian,* 10; Dio Cassius, *History,* 67.

a member of that noble family. While not impossible, it would seem more likely, since she was married to a Jew engaged in artisan work typical of the lower classes and moved about extensively with him, that the New Testament Prisca was a freed member of that household, and thus her name. Perhaps Aquila's Latin name was also an indication of freed status.

With reference to this couple in the New Testament, extraordinary interest has been devoted to the sequence in which their names are mentioned. In four of six references to them, Prisca is unconventionally named first (Acts 18:18, 26; Rom 16:3; 2 Tim 4:19). Many are convinced that this precedence given to Prisca indicates her greater social prominence, i.e., she was a member of a distinguished family who had married a Jew. However, the unlikelihood of that has just been noted. What is much more probable according to many commentators is that Prisca's mention before Aquila had to do with her missionary endeavors, i.e., she was the more active and better known missionary of the two.[19]

When Acts 18:2 first mentions Prisca and Aquila within the narrative about Paul founding the Church at Corinth around 50, it explains that they had moved from Rome to Corinth "because Claudius had commanded all the Jews to leave Rome." This is usually interpreted as an edict issued by Claudius in 49 whereby he sought to settle the turmoil among the Jews occasioned "at the instigation of Chrestus" by deporting the Jews.[20] This text shows that there must have been tensions in the Roman synagogues over the preaching of Jesus as Messiah. The expulsion of Prisca and Aquila from Rome would seem to indicate that they were involved to some extent with the Jesus movement before going to Corinth.[21] And, since there is never a hint that Paul converted them in Corinth nor that he exerted authority over them

---

[19]In Acts 18:26 the Western text (D) names Aquila first. See Bruce, *Pauline Circle*, 48, who attributes the change in order to the editor of D and comments that "he may have felt that it was unfitting that a woman should take the lead in a teaching ministry. Today some would put that editor down as a male chauvinist." On the alleged anti-feminism of the Western text, see above, pp. 26–27.

[20]Suetonius, *The Lives of the Twelve Caesars: Claudius,* 25. Most interpreters think Suetonius or the tradition upon which he relied had substituted "Chrestus" for "Christus" resulting from a confusion of vowels easily made in Latin.

[21]Bruce, *Pauline Circle*, 46, expresses agreement with Adolf Harnack, "Probabilia über die Adresse und den Verfasser des Hebraerbriefs," *ZNW* 1 (1900) 16–41, that Prisca and Aquila were founding members of the Roman Church.

during the years of their friendship as if they "owed him their own selves" (cf. Phlm 19), it is very likely they were already Christians before coming to Corinth. Furthermore, Paul refers in 1 Corinthians 16:15 to the household of Stephanas as the "first fruits of Achaia," people evidently converted after Prisca and her husband.[22] Hence Prisca and Aquila must have been converted before their acquaintance with Paul in Corinth.

It was shortly after their arrival in Corinth, where they had established themselves as tentmakers, that Prisca and Aquila met Paul, who had just come into the city for the first time. Such a meeting would have been quite natural since a stranger like Paul would normally have sought out those of the same ethnic and religious background, and even more so of the same occupation if he needed work.[23] Acts 18:3 comments that it was "because he was of the same trade" that Paul stayed with the Roman couple. Thus Prisca and Aquila became his hosts and probably in effect patrons by employing Paul.

A typical scene in a tentmaking shop has been described by Ronald Hock, who has investigated this occupation and its social context.[24] According to this author, in such shops tents were made from leather.[25] The atmosphere would have been quiet enough for a person to read or fall asleep. The workshop thus may well have been where Prisca,[26] Aquila, and Paul evangelized in the midst of their manual work together.[27] Prisca and her husband should not be thought of as primarily employers but as laborers themselves who had to work hard with their materials and who did not earn much; the wives in such laboring couples had to work with their husbands since the latter could not earn enough.[28] The most likely location for a shop of the type of Prisca's and Aquila's

[22]Although see above concerning Damaris and Dionysius the Areopagite as Paul's first Achaian converts, p. 27.

[23]See Meeks, *Urban Christians,* 29.

[24]See Hock, *Context,* 31–34.

[25]See *ibid.,* 21. Hock notes that while some have suggested tentmaking involved weaving tentcloth, the dominant view today is that it was a leatherworking trade (tanning not included).

[26]See above, p. 18 concerning Prisca's role in the shop.

[27]On the missionary use of a workshop, see Hock, *Context,* 37–42.

[28] Schottroff, "Women," 425.

was near the marketplace, a spot easily accessible to merchants, travelers, and city officials.

Prisca and Aquila left Corinth along with Paul after he had stayed there a year and six months (18:11). Acts does not tell the couple's reason for moving on (was it business or perhaps hostility such as Paul had encountered in Corinth?), nor does it mention how far they intended to travel with Paul whose own destination was Syria. It simply says that Paul left the couple in Ephesus (18:19). They apparently remained there for some years for in ca. 57 when Paul was again in Ephesus and writing from there to the Corinthians he included "hearty greetings in the Lord" from Aquila, Prisca, and "the church in their house" (1 Cor 16:19). It is significant that Paul refers to "their" house and not to "Aquila's" as one would expect given the tradition of the male as head of the household. This may hint at something about Paul's view of marriage partners as equals in Christ as well as about his perception of Prisca's importance as a leader in the Church.[29]

The religious prominence of this couple in Ephesus during those years is underscored in Acts. The narrative tells how they spent time with the itinerant Alexandrian preacher Apollos in order to complete his instruction in the faith. New to Ephesus, Apollos became known as an erudite and eloquent missionary who taught about Jesus, but who knew only about the baptism of John. For this reason, after hearing him speak, Prisca and Aquila "took him [*proselabonto autou*] and expounded to him the way of God more accurately" (Acts 18:26).[30] When Apollos soon after determined to go to Achaia, i.e., Corinth (18:27), Acts mentions that the Ephesian "brethren" (18:27), no doubt meaning Prisca,[31] Aquila and their house church, wrote recommending him to the disciples there.

[29]See Victor Paul Furnish, *The Moral Teaching of Paul. Selected Issues* (Nashville: Abingdon, 2nd ed. 1985) 105.

[30]According to C.E.B. Cranfield, *The Epistle to the Romans*. International Critical Commentary (Edinburgh: T & T Clark, 2 vols., 1975-79) II, 783, while it is possible that *proselabonto autou* has the sense of taking him aside in order to talk with him privately, it more probably means they received him in their home as a guest.

[31]See Fiorenza, "Missionaries," 427, who notes that since it is highly unlikely that the house church of Prisca and Aquila consisted solely of men, the exegete in a case like this must certainly read grammatically masculine (androcentrically oriented) language as inclusive, unless a case can be made to the contrary.

To Prisca's and Aquila's Ephesian period probably also belongs
an incident which stood out in Paul's memory, although Acts
seems not to allude to it. In Romans 16:3-4 Paul states that the
couple had "risked their necks for my life," a reference it would
seem to a time when Paul was in mortal danger. Was this during
the riot at Ephesus (cf. Acts 19:23-41)? During an imprisonment
there? No certainty can be established. What is clear, however,
is that if Romans 16:3 correctly reflects a return of Prisca and
Aquila to Rome,[32] something had influenced them, like Paul, to
leave Ephesus. While it may have been that under Nero the earlier expulsion of Jews by Claudius was no longer in effect, it may
also have been that the pair had been so shaken themselves by
the Ephesian situation in which they had helped Paul that they
too determined it was time to move on. Luise Schottroff has observed that whatever the particular circumstances were which
threatened Prisca and Aquila, "the assertions of Paul in Romans
16:3 show pointedly just what a dangerous life these congregations of Christians led, what an important role mutual solidarity
played, and that the women were just as much endangered as the
men in conflicts with the authorities."[33]

Back in Rome (ca. 58), as Paul's greetings to Prisca and Aquila
reveal in Romans 16:5, the house of the missionary couple again
became a center for Christian gatherings as it had been earlier
in Corinth and Ephesus. As Paul informed the Romans, not only
he owed Prisca and Aquila a debt of gratitude, "but also all the
churches of the Gentiles give thanks" (16:4). Clearly, the distinguished service of this rather nomadic missionary pair had made
them known and appreciated by many.

While in terms of social status Prisca and Aquila were most
likely freedpersons, they must also have been relatively well off.
They had been able to travel and to establish their small business
in several urban centers. Also, they supported not only themselves,
but hosted house churches wherever they went and missionaries
like Paul and Apollos. Travelling as a pair, they were not exceptional among Christians as Paul's remarks about married apostles

---

[32]While much debate has been given to the possibility that Romans 16 was originally
independent from the epistle and possibly first served as a letter to Ephesus, the current tide of opinion seems quite decided that it was an integral part of Paul's letter
to the Roman Church. See the brief discussion below, pp. 60-61.

[33]Schottroff, "Women," 425.

in 1 Corinthians 9:5 indicate. In this text where Paul has in mind his rights as an apostle, he observes: "Do we not have the right to be accompanied by a wife as the other apostles and the brothers of the Lord and Cephas?" Paul's question makes it clear that he (and Barnabas, cf. 9:6) was an exception to this practice. Paul uses a difficult double accusative, *adelphēn gunaika,* which is rendered merely as "wife" in the RSV text quoted here. A footnote in the RSV, however, gives "sister as wife" as the literal translation. But C. K. Barrett has questioned whether this is the best sense and proposed as an alternative "a wife who is a Christian sister."[34] The emphasis in his rendering would be on the apostle's right to travel with a wife. But then the qualification that she be a "Christian sister" appears superfluous unless the implication is that wives could accompany on the condition they were Christian. Since that hardly seems likely, probably to be preferred is the RSV phrasing "sister as wife." Here the stress is on the role of the woman as a sister, who is at the same time wife. Elisabeth Schüssler Fiorenza maintains that the meaning of this puzzling phrase is best clarified when "sister" like "brother" (cf. 1 Cor 1:1) is understood as a missionary co-worker.[35] In effect, therefore, Paul indicates that the widespread practice to which he was an exception was the missionary co-workers who were married couples. Fiorenza terms this "the practice of partnership-mission" which she says "appears to have been the rule in the Christian missionary movement, [and] which allowed for the equal participation of women with men in missionary work."[36]

It is significant to note that as Aquila's co-missionary, Prisca is never characterized by Paul as his wife. Rather, she is greeted (cf. Rom 16:3) or mentioned (cf. 1 Cor 16:9) because of her work as a Christian. None of the New Testament references to Prisca and Aquila in fact reflect overtones of patriarchy either in their

[34]Barrett, *First Corinthians,* 202–203.

[35]Fiorenza, "Missionaries," 431. She observes that a similar understanding is found as early as Clement of Alexandria, *Stromateis,* 3.6.53.3, who remarked that apostles "took their wives with them not as women with whom they had marriage relations but as sisters that they might be co-missionaries in dealing with housewives." In the case of Prisca (and Junia, see below, pp. 68–69), however, there is no indication her work was restricted to other women.

[36]*Ibid.*

community roles or in their own relationship. To the contrary, as remarked above, Prisca even emerges as the more prominent, the more active Christian. It is thus likely that the house churches she and Aquila formed were also relatively free from patriarchal dimensions.[37]

Just as Prisca's and Aquila's missionary work as a married couple was thereby not the same as Paul's, it has been suggested that their missionary method was also different:

> Insofar as they [Prisca and Aquila] . . . gathered converts in house churches, they did not divide the apostolic *diakonia* into the eucharistic table sharing that establishes community and the word that aims at the conversion of individuals. Insofar as Paul felt called "not to baptize but to preach the gospel," he did not concentrate on community building.[38]

Such an observation may point to a valid difference in *concentration* between the Christian work of Paul and that of Prisca and Aquila. Nonetheless, it would hardly be correct to imply that Paul was not vitally concerned about the upbuilding of the groups he had founded (cf. e.g., 1 Cor 12-14). Still, one does have the impression that, tentmakers though he, Prisca, and Aquila all were, Paul was given to singling out the disparate, dramatic, large and small "pieces" who joined his Churches whom he then left to Prisca and Aquila to sew together carefully into an entity called a house church.

The supposition that Prisca was more prominent in missionary endeavors than Aquila has led not only to the unverifiable theory already mentioned that she had come from a higher social status than her husband. It also has spawned the more probable proposal that since she is named first in the instruction of Apollos (Acts 18:26),[39] she must have been his primary teacher.[40] Enter-

---

[37]See Fiorenza, *In Memory,* 179. See also Gielen, "Zur Interpretation," 122-123, according to whose analysis the house church of Aquila and Priscilla referred to in 1 Corinthians 16:19 is not one among numerous other house churches in Ephesus, but was the whole local Church in that city. Gielen similarly characterizes the house church of the couple mentioned in Romans 16:5, an interpretation based on the assumption Romans 16 was originally an independent letter written elsewhere than to Rome.

[38]Fiorenza, *In Memory,* 179.

[39]Although not in Codex D. See above, p. 50, n. 1.

[40]On this basis Fiorenza, *In Memory,* 179, suggests that Apollos' "Sophia and Spirit theology might have been derived from her catechesis."

taining the thought of Prisca's theological expertise has led to the even further rather famous suggestion by Adolf Harnack that she was the anonymous author of the epistle to the Hebrews and that her name was omitted owing to prejudice against women teachers.[41] This idea, however, can hardly be supported.

While Prisca may never have authored an epistle, one can suppose that she and Aquila with their knowledge of the Roman situation, their Roman contacts, and their sustained association with Paul, may have informed and influenced him in his writing of the letter to the Romans (ca. 58). Perhaps behind the lofty dogmatic passages of Romans, the reader is really hearing echoes of concerns and discussions about the Roman Church and pertinent issues there voiced by Prisca and Aquila to Paul.

The last facet of the story of Prisca and Aquila reflected in the New Testament is a greeting to them in 2 Timothy 4:19 which, if historically reliable, would place them in Ephesus again in the mid to late 60s. Is this possible, another move? Some would suggest that the statement of 2 Timothy 4:19 in effect challenges Rome as the destination of Romans 16, that in fact Romans 16 must have been sent to Ephesus, and thus that Prisca and Aquila had remained there since 51. Yet others point out that the nomadic character of the couple's life was not uncharacteristic of Jews of the day and that this in itself does not challenge Rome as the destination of chapter 16. Following the latter assumption, the path of Prisca's and Aquila's moves thus goes from Rome to Corinth (ca. 49), to Ephesus (ca. 51), back to Rome (ca. 57), and then back to Ephesus (mid to late 60s).

The New Testament gives no hint of the later years of this couple. What remains a puzzle is whether there was a final return to Rome. Post-New Testament traditions certainly support that by the various links drawn between Prisca, Aquila, and the Roman Church of St. Prisca on the Aventine.[42] For example, the tenth-century *Acts of St. Prisca* state that the body of the saint was moved from where she had been buried on the Ostian road to the church on the Aventine. And a tenth-century inscription,

---

[41]Harnack, "Probabilia," 16–17.

[42]The most detailed discussion of these traditions remains the note on Aquila and Priscilla in William Sanday and Arthur Headlam, *The Epistle to the Romans.* International Critical Commentary (Edinburgh: T & T Clark, 5th ed. 1902) 418–420.

which was formerly over the door of the church, identifies the
spot as the house of Prisca and Aquila. But that evidence, along
with numerous other traditions not mentioned here, is very late
and most likely represents a longing to connect the spot with the
New Testament Church.

The lives of Euodia, Syntyche, and Prisca offer a fleeting
glimpse of three women whom Paul called "co-workers," and
perhaps at least one suggestion about the women who encountered Paul in that role: In the case of each of these three, a
"strong" type of personality confronts us.

With Euodia and Syntyche, we see two Church members, evidently leaders, who had not easily given up their public differences, a situation they let perdure under the scrutiny of their
Church. One wonders if even Paul's admonition was able to help
resolve their differences.

With Prisca we find a similar character type, a women who was
perceived as more dominant than her husband, a person who had
developed several house churches and one who must have had
no qualms about correcting a popular visiting preacher.

While no information comes to us about the interaction of these
women with Paul, what does speak loudly is both Paul's continual
involvement with them and the gratitude and appreciation he expresses for them. Clearly, in both cases Paul had collaborated
with these people over a long period of time. Obviously, then,
women who were of a very determined cast, at least as represented
by these three, found themselves able to co-exist in Christian mission and work along with Paul. Given that Paul himself had a
forceful personality, that he was aggressive and fearless in public
confrontation (cf. Gal 2), one might suspect that he would have
preferred more docile and demure female co-workers. Yet, of
course, the choice of whose life was touched by the Spirit was
hardly his; the role of the divine cannot be overlooked. Furthermore, because Paul viewed partnership with his co-workers as
based on the gospel, a point underscored by the important study
of Ollrog,[43] what really mattered to Paul and his collaborators
was preaching and ministering, not observing hierarchy among

[43]See above, pp. 43-45.

themselves. With such a focus on ministering to the needs of others, the collaboration and mutual appreciation of even very strong personalities was apparently enabled.

Is this not a challenge for Churches today, especially those in which male-dominated leadership sometimes clashes with other Church members, often very energetic, determined females attempting to respond to needs in ministry? Should the focus of Christians not be on the gospel and the needs of God's people rather than on asserting and preserving authority, power, and rank? Should not all "lording it over each other" be abolished in the Lord's service and ways made possible for the collaboration and mutual appreciation among all those called to be co-workers?

5

A Deacon and an Apostle:
Phoebe and Junia

Of all the women who knew Paul, two who receive a great amount of attention in contemporary biblical literature are Phoebe and Junia. The reason is evident: They are described by Paul, respectively, with the titles of deacon and apostle, terms which suggest they held significant ministerial and leadership roles in the early Church. But these same terms cause modern Christians to wonder why women in Christianity today, particularly in Roman Catholicism, are in contrast excluded from most leadership and official ministerial positions. If then, why not now?

This major issue of the role of women in Church leadership, the discussion and resolution of which is at varying stages in the numerous Christian denominations, has led many to scrutinize Phoebe and Junia. Under such examination these women emerge as most interesting.

Phoebe

Phoebe was a member of the Church at Cenchreae, a seaport seven miles east of Corinth on the Saronic Gulf.[1] Her name, an

On Phoebe see especially Fiorenza, "Missionaries," 423-427; Gerhard Lohfink, "Weibliche Diakone im Neuen Testament," *Diakonia* 11 (1980) 385-400, 388-391; Margaret Howe, *Women and Church Leadership* (Grand Rapids: Zondervan, 1982) 30-34; Robert Jewett, "Paul, Phoebe and the Spanish Mission," in Jacob Neusner *et al* (eds.), *The Social World of Formative Christianity and Judaism: Essays in Tribute to Howard Clark Kee* (Philadelphia: Fortress, 1988) 142-161.

epithet for the goddess Artemis, suggests she must have been a Gentile since it is unlikely to have been given to a Jewess. Phoebe's memory has been preserved solely on the basis of a recommendation Paul wrote for her at the beginning of the final chapter of Romans:

> I [Paul] commend to you our sister Phoebe, a deaconess of the church at Cenchreae, that you may receive her in the Lord as befits the saints, and help her in whatever she may require from you, for she has been a helper of many and of myself as well (Rom 16:1-2).

Before this information can be examined, some discussion of the text critical problem of Romans 16 is in order. Briefly put, because the doxology in 16:25-27 is variously located in the manuscripts of Romans, and because some manuscripts omit chapter 16 entirely, the question has arisen whether this chapter was part of the original text of Romans. Much of the scholarship devoted to this issue has concluded that chapter 16 was in fact a later addition, e.g., a letter of greetings sent to the Ephesians along with a copy of a fifteen-chapter Romans. Among the problems this judgment intended to resolve was the question of how Paul could have sent greetings to so many people in a Church he had never visited (Rome).

Ephesus seemed to be a more fitting destination for chapter 16. But recent discussions of the integrity of Romans have swung back to the opinion that Romans 16 was included originally with the previous fifteen chapters.[2] One point stressed is that the greetings in chapter 16 are actually inappropriate for Ephesus or any other Church setting which Paul supposedly knew well. The personal details Paul cites with respect to some of the people he greets sound as if the letter's hearers as a whole do not themselves know these people well. Rather, it appears Paul is introducing or recommending those he greets, hoping they will be given more recognition in a group where neither he nor they are very well known.

The debate about Romans 16, which is far more complex than

---

[2]Most influential has been the study by Harry Gamble, *The Textual History of the Letter to the Romans: A Study in Textual and Literary Criticism* (Grand Rapids: Eerdmans, 1977).

what has been sketchily outlined here,[3] is relevant to any interest in Phoebe since the destination of Romans 16 accords with the travel and introduction of Phoebe. And, to know where Phoebe was going is perhaps to be enlightened about her purpose for travelling.

The proponents of the Ephesian hypothesis assume that she was moving to Ephesus or journeying there on business and that Paul was paving the way for the Ephesian Church's reception of her. Advocates of a Roman destination for chapter 16, of course, think Phoebe was going to Rome. It is important to note that from either perspective there is general agreement that Phoebe was the bearer of the letter introducing her. Our assumption here is that chapter 16 was indeed integral to Paul's original epistle to the Romans and that Phoebe carried the entire document with her as she set off from Cenchreae to the Imperial City.

Because chapter 16 opens with Paul's commendation of Phoebe, it is evident that she and her mission in Rome were of great importance to Paul. In asking the Romans to be hospitable to Phoebe, he describes her using three titles: *adelphē,* "sister," *diakonos,* "deacon," and *prostatis,* "patroness." For Paul to call Phoebe "our[4] sister" indicates that she was a Christian. The specification that she was a *diakonos* of the Church at Cenchreae appears to give her a qualification beyond being a sister.[5]

In fairness to Paul's Greek, in which *diakonos* may be either masculine or feminine, Phoebe should be called a deacon, not a deaconess as in the RSV translation quoted above. To describe her as a deaconess is, first, to imply that Paul used a term, *diakonissa,* which does not appear in Greek during the period of Pauline Christianity and, second, to suggest, in view of the later and modern deaconess movements, that Phoebe's role was subordinate to that of male deacons and involved primarily ministry to other

[3]On various aspects related to the discussion, see Karl P. Donfried (ed.), *The Romans Debate* (Minneapolis: Augsburg, 1977).

[4]"Your" appears in a few manuscripts, e.g., P[46] A G, but it is probably traceable to scribal error.

[5]The term *diakonos* is preceded by a variant, an emphatic *kai,* "and," "also," in e.g., P[46] B C. Jewett, "Phoebe," 159, n. 53, judges that "it has a slightly condescending effect, suggesting that her status as deacon improves her rank as a mere 'sister,' and thus is less likely to have originated with Paul than with later, more chauvinistic traditions."

women. Paul, however, indicates no subordination or restrictions due to gender in Phoebe's role. In his view she is simply and unequivocally, "deacon of the church at Cenchreae."

The term "deacon" was one rather frequently used by Paul. In Philippians 1:1 he addresses "bishops and deacons." Here the reference, not attached to any specific individuals, quite evidently names officeholders within the Christian community. Because in the context of the letter Paul is thanking the Philippians for material assistance, the bishops and deacons to whom he refers were probably people who in their ministry were responsible for collecting and sending what Paul had needed.[6] Elsewhere when Paul uses *diakonos* it describes his co-workers and assistants in evangelization (so Apollos in 1 Cor 3:5; Timothy in 1 Thess 3:2, cf. 1 Tim 4:6; cf. Tychicus in Col 4:7; Eph 6:21; cf. Epaphras in Col 1:7), his own ministry (1 Cor 3:5; 2 Cor 3:6; 6:4; 11:23; cf. Col 1:23, 25; Eph 3:7), the ministry of Christ (Rom 15:8; Gal 2:17), or even the work of civil authorities (Rom 13:4). In the majority of these instances *diakonos* is translated by the RSV as "servant" or "minister,"[7] all the references assumably being to males. This survey makes it clear that Phoebe has been discriminated against in, for example, the RSV rendering. Why not call her "servant" or "minister" also? Why set her apart into the anachronistic category of deaconess? As Margaret Howe has observed, "The translators of the RSV have left the impression that Phoebe's office was in some way different from that of her male colleagues. And because in the contemporary church setting the title 'minister' is more prestigious than that of 'deacon,' Phoebe is placed a little lower on the scale of values than is actually warranted by the text."[8] As many scholars have pointed out, such denigration of Phoebe is no longer tolerable.[9] This issue serves as a striking example that translations can reflect the preconceived notions of the translators.

---

[6] There is no reason to be certain, as some interpreters seem to be, that women were not among these officeholders, especially given the history of the earliest Philippian Christian community. See above on Lydia, p. 29, and concerning Euodia and Syntyche, p. 46. Another possible New Testament reference to women deacons is found in 1 Timothy 3:11, although some hold that the text is directed to wives of male deacons.

[7] Galatians 2:17 is the exception where *diakonos* is rendered "agent."

[8] Howe, *Women*, 31–32.

[9] See Fiorenza, *In Memory*, 170–171.

That Paul recognized Phoebe as a deacon on a par with the others, and himself, as Paul uses the term, raises questions about Phoebe's precise role. What was her ministry? Since Paul's numerous uses of *diakonos* for himself and the various male co-workers noted above basically portray them as missionaries entrusted with preaching and ministering within churches,[10] the same must be assumed of Phoebe. She was evidently a teacher and missionary in the Church of Cenchreae. In view of the possessive expression "deacon of the church," however, it is probable that she functioned as a local rather than an itinerant leader.[11]

It is instructive to note that Paul appears to equate *diakonos* with *synergos,* "co-worker" (cf. 1 Cor 3:5-9; 2 Cor 6: 1, 4) and in one case to use *diakonos* interchangeably with *apostolos,* "apostle" (2 Cor 11:13-15).[12] Therefore it can be assumed that in calling Phoebe a deacon Paul understood her to have a specific Church role as did the other women and men he variously calls co-workers and apostles.[13]

While Phoebe's ministry as a deacon has inspired and continues to inspire much discussion, her role as a *prostatis* is also being given close scrutiny. That term, a feminine noun found in the New Testament only here, literally means "one who stands before," thus "patroness, protectress." Its masculine counterpart, *prostatēs,* has the technical sense of a legal patron. It has been argued by Ernst Käsemann, however, that in Phoebe's case the term "cannot in the context have the juridical sense of the masculine form, i.e., the leader or representative of a fellowship" since women could not take on legal functions.[14] Rather, "the idea is

[10]See Ollrog, *Mitarbeiter,* 73-74.

[11]So Jewett, "Phoebe," 149.

[12]Cf. Elisabeth Schüssler Fiorenza, "The Apostleship of Women in Early Christianity," in Leonard and Arlene Swidler (eds.), *Women Priests. A Catholic Commentary on the Vatican Declaration* (New York: Paulist, 1977) 135-140, 137.

[13]See Mary Ann Getty, "God's Fellow Workers and Apostleship," in Swidler, *Women Priests,* 176-182. Cf. Ellis, "Co-Workers," 442-445, who argues that *diakonoi* were a special class of co-workers who taught and preached and were entitled to support by the community. Analogously he understands *apostoloi* as a special class of *diakonoi,* who did the same work as the *diakonoi* but who had the important distinction of having had a dominical commission. But as Meeks, *Urban Christians,* 234, n. 73, has observed, Ellis' divisions are "too brittle." It is not at all certain that Paul's language so precisely sorts out distinct functional classes of co-workers.

[14]Ernst Käsemann, *Commentary on Romans.* trans. and ed. by G. W. Bromiley from German 4th ed. (Grand Rapids: Eerdmans, 1980) 411.

that of the personal care which Paul and others have received at the hands of the deaconess."[15] But in response to Käsemann, Fiorenza has observed:

> It is obvious that an androcentric perspective on early Christian history has to explain away the meaning of both words [*diakonos* and *prostatis*], because it does not allow for women in church leadership, or it can accord them only "feminine" assisting functions. Since this traditional interpretive model takes it for granted that the leadership of the early church was in the hands of men, it assumes that the women mentioned in the Pauline letters were the helpers and assistants of the male apostles and missionaries, especially of Paul. Such an androcentric model of historical reconstruction cannot imagine or conceptualize that women such as Phoebe could have had leadership equal to and sometimes even superior to men in early Christian beginnings.

Also advanced in refutation of Käsemann's explanation is some recently published information from the Greco-Roman period noted by Robert Jewett which indicates that in fact women were appointed in many instances to the role of a *prostatis,* a legal patron.[16] For example, numerous women are known to have served as the protectors and donors of *collegia,* associations.

In light of these observations, how then is Phoebe's role to be envisioned? Certainly Paul's statement that she was a patroness both to him and to "many" (16:2) indicates a level of material resources which points to a high social standing, namely, to a role as an upperclass benefactor of the local Christian community. Probably Phoebe had a house large enough to accommodate Church gatherings where she hosted the meetings and exercised her leadership role as *diakonos.* In relation to her as such a key member of the Church of Cenchreae, as Jewett assesses it, Paul would have had a "relatively subordinate social position as her client." This leads him to comment further that it is thus "preposterous that translations like the RSV render *prostatis* as 'helper.' "[17]

[15]*Ibid.*

[16]Jewett, "Phoebe," 149.

[17]Jewett, "Phoebe," 150. An early, often cited protest against this translation is Margaret D. Gibson's "Phoebe," *Expository Times* 23 (1911–12) 281.

Paul's commendation of Phoebe in Romans 16:1-2 inspires discussion not only about her role in the Cenchreaen group but also about her purposes in going to Rome. It has generally been assumed that while Phoebe was evidently delivering Paul's letter, this must have coincided with other reasons for such major travel, perhaps a business trip. However, a new theory has been proposed which is bound to reopen debate. Jewett has advanced the idea that Phoebe's real mission in Rome was to persuade the Church there to support Paul's planned evangelization of Spain. Why? Because Phoebe "had agreed to cooperate with Paul as the patroness of the Spanish mission."[18]

Jewett introduces his theory by showing that the Spanish mission could not proceed in the manner of Paul's usual strategy, since there were few Jews in Spain and Paul would furthermore have had language problems. He surmises that Phoebe therefore went to Rome while Paul was delivering the Jerusalem collection, and made it her task to create the logistical base for the Spanish evangelization, i.e. to enlist the support of the Roman Christians.

Jewett draws his theory essentially from two phrases in Paul's commendation of Phoebe in Romans 16:2: "Receive her in the Lord as befits the saints," and "help her in whatever she may require from you." He interprets the first, particularly in view of Phoebe's role as a *diakonos* and a *prostatis,* to imply that Phoebe should be received with honor befitting her social class, her role as a Church leader, her previous benefactions to Christian mission, and her role in the planned Spanish project. The second half of the request Jewett renders (in contrast to the RSV cited above) as "provide her whatever she needs from you in the matter [*pragmati*].[19] In his view, the "matter" is Phoebe's patronage of the Spanish mission.

While Jewett's fascinating theory about Phoebe certainly has an air of possibility about it, the question is whether it is probable. And that is where an impasse is reached. Just as there is little in Paul's remarks which could be cited to refute Jewett's idea, there is also nothing compelling to support it beyond his own reading of Romans 16:2 and an application to the context

---

[18]Jewett, "Phoebe," 151.

[19]*Ibid.*, 150. Cf. Cranfield, *Romans,* 782, whose literal translation is "assist her in any matter in which she may need your help."

of Spain at the time. In the end, however, Jewett whether he is correct or not adds an important dimension to analyses of Phoebe. He, along with others who argue for a non-patriarchal understanding of her roles as a deacon and a patroness, contributes much to destroying portrayals which prejudicially confined Phoebe to being simply a helpful woman from the Cenchreaen Christian community who as a dependent female needed whatever hospitality the Roman Christians might charitably extend to her. To the contrary, the Phoebe we now see had resources, a respectable social status, a leadership position in her Church, and Paul and many others were indebted to her. Undoubtedly such a person went to Rome with a definite agenda and the means to carry it out. Jewett's creative analysis stimulates us to continue to ponder just what that was.

Junia

Another leader in the early Church who knew Paul, and whom many are convinced must have been a woman (contrary to the RSV quoted here), is mentioned by Paul in the closing chapter of his epistle to the Romans:[20]

> Greet Andronicus and Junias [*Iounian*], my kinsmen and my fellow-prisoners; they are men of note among the apostles, and they were in Christ before me (16:7).

No one disputes that Andronicus is a masculine name, but the gender of the person named *Iounian*[21] has occasioned much disagreement. Confusion arises because the Greek *Iounian* is the accusative form which could indicate either the feminine name Junia or the masculine Junias. The masculine could be either an uncontracted name or a contraction of Junianus. Arguments have been advanced to support reading either gender, although the stronger case is decidedly in favor of the feminine.[22]

[20]On the destination of Romans 16, see above, pp. 60–61.

[21]A few mss., e.g., P⁴⁶, read *Ioulian*, Julia, but this is generally rejected as a scribal error probably made under the influence of Romans 16:15. See Metzger, *Textual Commentary*, 539.

[22]The most detailed analysis of these grammatical considerations is by Ray R. Schulz, "Romans 16:7: Junia or Junias?" *Expository Times* 98 (1987) 108–110. On the whole issue of the identity of Junia see also Bernadette Brooten, "Junia . . . Outstanding

While much attention has been given to how the name is accented in the Greek text (*Iouníav* with an acute favoring a female name, *Iouniân* with a circumflex indicating a contracted male name), accents cannot be finally decisive since they were not added to Greek manuscripts until the Middle Ages. What is of special interest, however, is the testimony of patristic writers. Because they read an unaccented text, which they interpreted on the basis of context and grammar, and because many such writers spoke Greek themselves, their understanding carries a heavy weight. In a survey of Church Fathers up to the twelfth century who commented on Romans 16:7, the overwhelming consensus was to give a feminine reading.[23] One of the most striking comments is that by Chrysostom. Of Junia he wrote: "Oh! How great is the devotion of this woman, that she should be counted worthy of the appellation of the apostle!"[24]

From the ninth and tenth centuries, when accents were imposed on the Greek texts, Greek New Testaments marked *Iounian* with the acute, thus favoring a feminine interpretation.[25] Only in this century has a change occurred with most Greek New Testaments now printing a circumflex, implying a contracted male name.[26] And, most English translations today, as the RSV cited above, read Junias rather than Junia.

In support of the masculine reading it has been said that a contracted name would fit well in the Romans 16 list of greetings where three other contractions ending in -*as,* all masculine, are included: Patrobas, Hermas, and Olympas (16:4-5). It has also been argued that since Paul identifies the person in question along with Andronicus as an apostle, Paul must have been referring to a male. But this latter approach belies a prejudice, a presupposition not found, for example, in ancient writers like Chrysostom.

Among the Apostles (Rom 16:7)," in Swidler, *Women Priests,* 141-144; Lohfink, "Weibliche Diakone," 391-395; Cranfield, *Romans,* 788-790; Howe, *Women,* 34-36; Valentin Fabrega, "War Junia(s) der hervorragende Apostel (Rom 16, 7), eine Frau?" *Jahrbuch für Antike und Christentum* 27/28 (1984-85) 47-64; Peter Lampe, "Iunia/ Iunias: Sklavenherkunft im Kreise der vorpaulinischen Apostel (Rom 16, 7)," *Zeitschrift für die neutestamentliche Wissenschaft* 76 (1985) 132-134.

[23]See Schulz, "Romans 16:6," 109; Fabrega, "Junia(s)," 54-64.

[24]Chrysostom, *Epistle to the Romans,* Homily 31.

[25]So Schulz, "Romans 16:6," 109.

[26]So *ibid.*

What tips the balance most decisively toward a feminine reading, however, is not so much opinion but the fact that Junia was a common Roman female name, while not a single instance of the masculine Junias either contracted or uncontracted is attested.[27]

On the likelihood that Paul was greeting a woman, Junia, along with Andronicus, we can suppose that they were a married couple (or, although it seems less likely, brother and sister). Paul's description of them as his kinsmen and their Greek (Andronicus) and Latin (Junia) names indicate that they were probably Hellenistic Jews like Paul himself. Peter Lampe argues that Junia must have been originally of servile origin or born of parents who were. He bases this on her name, which was unusual for someone of Jewish origin, and asserts that it would only have been given to someone connected with a male named Junius, assumably her or her parents' patron or former owner.[28]

Paul describes Junia and Andronicus as having been his "fellow prisoners," which may mean they were in the same prison together (where is not evident) or perhaps they, like Paul, had also known imprisonment because of Christ. He further characterizes them as being "of note among the apostles" (the "men" of the RSV's "men of note" is not in the Greek). While a few have interpreted this to mean that they were well-known to the apostles, most judge it far more likely that the phrase means they were distinguished as apostles themselves.[29] The term apostle thus has a broader sense here than the Twelve (or the Eleven faithful plus Matthias) as it does in numerous other texts (e.g., Acts 14:4, 14; 1 Cor 12:28; Eph 4:11). Such apostles were essentially itiner-

---

[27]See Fabrega, "Junia(s)," 48–49.

[28]Lampe, "Sklavenherkunft," 132–133. Lampe leaves open the question of the gender of Junia(s) and maintains that his theory of servile origin would be true of either a male or female.

[29]See Rudolf Schnackenburg, "Apostles Before and During Paul's Time," in W. Ward Gasque and Ralph P. Martin (eds.), *Apostolic History and the Gospel. Biblical and Historical Essays Presented to F. F. Bruce on His 60th Birthday.* (Grand Rapids: Eerdmans, 1970) 287–303, 293. This article offers an analysis of Paul's use of the term apostle, although it assumes without discussion the male gender of Junia(s). Cf. Schulz, "Romans 16:7," 109, whose survey of Church Fathers found "they . . . agree that 'of note among the apostles' means 'noted apostles' and not 'noted in the estimation of the apostles.' " So also Cranfield, *Romans,* 789.

ant missionaries[30] who spread the gospel and were recognized in the Churches as a rather distinct group of leaders (see esp. 1 Cor 12:28, Eph 4:11). Some assume that Junia and Andronicus belonged to a group of apostles, heralds of the gospel, and were so recognized by persons like Paul even though they could not lay claim to an appearance of the risen Lord.[31] Others think that these two could in fact have belonged to the circle of apostles in Jerusalem who, along with James, had had a vision of the resurrected Lord.[32] While it is not possible to judge which was the case, in light of the general suppression of women's leadership throughout later Church history, it is appropriate to stress here that Paul has not only mentioned Junia as one of these apostles but has also described her as *outstanding* among them.

A last important piece of information Paul gives about Junia and Andronicus is that they were "in Christ" before he was. Since Paul himself was converted rather early, this pair must have belonged to the Christian community in its very earliest days.[33] As Hellenistic Jews, perhaps they had been residents of Jerusalem like Barnabas or at least visitors there. Maybe they were members of Stephen's synagogue and among those dispersed in the persecution following his death (Acts 11:19). Perhaps they were also among the first Christians to evangelize in Antioch[34] or Rome. In any case, clearly the apostle Junia and her partner Andronicus had been impressively active so that they had come to be greatly appreciated by Paul. They stand along with another famous pair, Prisca and Aquila, as witnesses to the missionary work of married Christians, and as already mentioned,[35] in that respect they were joined by many others.

The influence of Phoebe and Junia has extended far beyond the early days of Christianity into discussions about the role of women in the modern Church. Clearly, on many accounts, the

---

[30]See Schnackenburg, "Apostles," 294.

[31]See *ibid.*, 294.

[32]Fiorenza, *In Memory*, 172.

[33]See Schnackenburg, "Apostles," 293-294.

[34]So Ollrog, *Mitarbeiter*, 51-52.

[35]See above, pp. 53-55, and below, p. 75.

Churches Phoebe and Junia knew were vastly different from ours. That appears so especially on the level of leadership and full participation by women. There is absolutely no hint in the New Testament that Phoebe and Junia, nor any other woman, had to struggle to be able to exercise her ministry. Nor is there the least suggestion on the part of Paul as he mentions these people that as women in their roles they were at all exceptional. Thus it can be concluded safely that Phoebe and Junia as women leaders, a deacon and an apostle, are but two examples of numerous women who must have also had these roles. If only the history of Christian origins knew the names and stories of those many others whom Phoebe and Junia typify. What fascinating chapters must be missing from our history.

6

Workers in the Lord
and Other Church Members:
Mary, Tryphaena and Tryphosa, Persis,
the Mother of Rufus, Julia and the Sister of Nereus,
Claudia, Apphia,
the Daughters of Philip, Mary and Rhoda of Jerusalem

A major problem with attempting to categorize or group together the women who knew Paul is that neat and comprehensive divisions are not really possible. In this section it will be especially clear that the women included are not linked by any one theme. Rather, they are those about whom there is very little to be said individually. Yet they are interesting for our consideration because of their presence in the New Testament and their awareness of Paul. First we will treat a number of women known only from brief greetings to them by Paul in Romans 16: Mary, Tryphaena, Tryphosa, Persis, the mother of Rufus, Julia, and the sister of Nereus. Then Claudia, followed by Apphia will be examined. Finally, some women referred to in Acts, namely, the daughters of Philip, Mary of Jerusalem and her servant Rhoda, whom it appears also knew Paul will be briefly discussed.

Mary, Tryphaena and Tryphosa, Persis,
the Mother of Rufus, Julia and the Sister of Nereus

Paul's greetings to the Roman Christians in Romans 16:3-23[1] are for us a source of names and some details about people, espe-

On the destination of this chapter, see above, pp. 60–61.

cially women, who either knew him or whom he had heard of.[2] Nine women, clearly all Christians, are included among the twenty-six individuals mentioned by name in the greetings.[3] The women, like the men, are characterized by their labors or membership in the various Roman congregations or house churches, with no apparent ranking between the men and women being suggested. Of the women mentioned, we have already described Prisca (16:3-5) and Junia (16:7). The other seven are: Mary (16:6), Tryphaena and Tryphosa (16:12), Persis (16:12), the mother of Rufus (16:13), Julia and the sister of Nereus (16:15).[4]

Mary, Tryphaena, Tryphosa, and Persis have the distinction of being referred to by Paul as "workers." Paul describes them with terminology based on the verb *kopiaō*, "to labor" or "to toil," which he elsewhere employs to designate his own activity of evangelization and teaching (1 Cor 4:12, 15:10; Gal 4:11; Phil 2:16; 1 Thess 5:12). Thus, these women stood out in Paul's memory or in what he heard about them because of their efforts on behalf of the gospel.

Mary is sent greetings by Paul with an observation of praise added that she had "worked hard [*polla ekopiasen*] among you [*eis humas*]" (16:6).[5] It is not evident whether her name is Jewish or Gentile since manuscript evidence diverges with some witnesses giving the Hebrew "Mariam"[6] and others "Marian,"[7] which could be either a Hellenized form of the Hebrew name or the feminine form of the Roman name "Marius." Consequently, whether Mary was a Jewish or a Gentile Christian is difficult to assess.

---

[2]It is possible Paul knew some of the individuals or groups mentioned in Romans 16 only by reputation; some he obviously knew personally, probably having met them during their travels or years of living in the East. See Meeks, *Urban Christians,* 56.

[3]For analyses of the persons in Romans 16, see e.g., Cranfield, *Romans,* 780-808; Fiorenza, Missionaries, *passim.* See also especially Sanday and Headlam, *Romans,* 416-432, whose comments give detailed attention to the appearance of these persons' names in Roman and Greek inscriptions, most notably in those from the imperial household.

[4]Of these, Meeks, *Urban Christians,* 56, 60, judges that Paul had known personally only the mother of Rufus.

[5]The reading *eis hēmas,* "among us," found e.g., in L, is judged to be a later change. Cranfield, *Romans,* 787, observes that Mary's "much labouring was for the good of the Roman Christians, not a service rendered specially to Paul and his companions."

[6]E.g., P⁴⁶ K D.

[7]E.g., A B C.

It has been argued that she must have been a Gentile since Paul does not describe her as his kinswoman (cf. 16:7, 11, 21), but this is not convincing since, for example, Aquila, who is known from Acts 18:2 to have been a Jew is not so characterized by Paul either. Tryphaena and Tryphosa are greeted together as "workers in the Lord" [*tas kopiōsas en kyrio*] (16:12). Their names, not uncommon in either Greek or Latin, are rooted in the Greek term *truphē*, "softness, delicacy, daintiness." An irony between their names and their labors in the Lord may have been apparent to Paul and his readers. Because of the similarity in their names and the fact that Paul mentions them in one breath, it has been generally assumed that they were sisters, perhaps even twins. It is also possible that they were two unrelated women who were associated together because of the similarity of their names.

In later Christian tradition a Tryphaena is also named in the apocryphal *Acts of Paul*. There she is a queen, a rich Christian widow from Pisidian Antioch who gives Paul money for the poor and offers hospitality to Thecla. It is known that in fact there was a queen of Pontus named Tryphaena who was a contemporary of Paul and a distant relative of the reigning Claudians.[8] This does not accord with the *Acts of Paul,* however, which says that she lived in Antioch of Pisidia. It has been suggested, nevertheless, that Christians joined together in oral tradition both their memory of the queen of Pontus and their awareness of Tryphaena in Romans 16:12, one known to have worked with Paul. The result is the queen Tryphaena of the apocryphal document who was envisioned as sympathetic to his cause.[9] If that speculation is accurate, and it is probable, it sheds some light on the Tryphaena of the apocryphal *Acts,* but unfortunately adds nothing to what is known of the person greeted in Romans 16:12. It does reflect, however, the esteem with which early Christians recalled this person.

Persis, also mentioned by Paul in Romans 16:12, receives an especially warm greeting in the context. Paul describes her as "the beloved" who had "worked hard [*polla ekopiasen*] in the Lord" (16:12). Persis was probably a slave or a freedwoman since her

---

[8]So Dennis R. MacDonald, *The Legend and the Apostle. The Battle for Paul in Story and in Canon* (Philadelphia: Westminster, 1983) 20-21.

[9]See *ibid.*

name, meaning "a Persian woman,"[10] is a typical Greek slave name often found in papyri and inscriptions.

In addition to Mary, Tryphaena, Tryphosa, and Persis, there are three other women to be noted here as mentioned by Paul in Romans 16. One is a person whom Paul identifies simply as the mother of Rufus. In 16:13 Paul greets Rufus, described as "eminent in the Lord," and then his mother whom Paul affectionately says was "his mother and mine." We have already noted[11] that Paul's special claim to this woman probably means that she had at some time been his benefactress or hostess.

A number of proposed connections have been suggested relating this woman and her son to other New Testament traditions. For example, it has been observed that in Mark 15:21, Simon of Cyrene is named as the father of Alexander and Rufus. On the assumption that the Markan Rufus and the Rufus of Romans 16:13 are the same,[12] the latter's mother might therefore have been the wife of Simon of Cyrene. A further suggestion is that the Markan Simon is in fact the Antiochian resident Symeon, surnamed Niger in Acts 13:1. This has led finally to the idea that Paul perhaps lodged in Antioch with this family and during that period experienced the mother of Rufus as "mother" to him also. But these are all speculative linkings with little or nothing to support them.

The final women to be mentioned who are named by Paul in Romans 16 are Julia and the sister of Nereus. These two are included with others in 16:15 where Paul writes: "Greet Philologus, Julia, Nereus and his sister, and Olympas, and all the saints who are with them."

Because Julia is named with Philologus, she is supposed by some to have been his wife (or sister), with Nereus, his sister and Olympas possibly being their children. Since Philologus was a common slave name, this family, or these associated individuals were probably all of that status. Julia was the most common of all Roman female names and while it was widely given to free

---

[10]See above concerning Lydia's name, p. 31.

[11]See above, p. 19.

[12]Cf. the observation by Raymond Brown in Raymond Brown and John Meier, *Antioch and Rome. New Testament Cradles of Catholic Christianity* (New York: Paulist, 1983) 197, who describes this identification as "adventurous."

women of the *gens Julia,* it is also known to have been the name most often used among slaves in the imperial household.[13]

It is debatable whether by the "sister" of Nereus Paul meant his sibling, his Christian wife, or his co-missionary. Fiorenza thinks that insofar as "sister" here might be, as elsewhere, a designation of Christian role, Nereus and his sister, along with Philologus and Julia, could be two more missionary couples like Prisca and Aquila and Junia and Andronicus.[14] That is a possibility, but one cannot be certain.

While the above remarks may seem to offer an inclusive survey of all the women Paul had in mind as he wrote Romans 16, as we noted earlier, grammatically masculine but inclusive language in the text of the epistle in fact suggests that Paul was aware of various other women in the Roman house churches.[15] For instance, among those who belonged to "the family of Aristobulus" (16:10) and "the family of Narcissus" (16:11) surely there were women. Likewise, the "brethren" and "saints" with those greeted in 16:14-15 must have included females. Furthermore, the house church of Prisca and Aquila (16:5) was very likely a mixed group. Thus it is apparent that many more women in Rome knew or at least knew of Paul than Romans 16 at first glance suggests.

Claudia

Another woman associated with Roman Christianity, although she is not mentioned in Romans 16, is Claudia. This person is portrayed in 2 Timothy 4:21 as being in contact with Paul during the imprisonment referred to in that letter and during which he supposedly wrote it. On the likelihood that there might be some historical basis connecting Paul with those named in the Pastorals, this would place Claudia as having lived in Rome, although Caesarea has also been defended. Claudia, along with Pudens and Linus, after whom she is mentioned, sends greetings to Timothy. Her name suggests that she was of the *gens Claudia* or perhaps belonged in some other capacity to the imperial household, maybe as a slave.

---

[13]See Sanday and Headlam, *Romans* 427; Cranfield, *Romans,* 795.

[14]Fiorenza, *In Memory,* 180. See also above, pp. 53–55, 69, and below, pp. 77–78.

[15]So Fiorenza, "Missionaries," 427.

The *Apostolic Constitutions* 7.46, a late fourth-century collection of ecclesiastical law, states that a certain *Linos ho Klaudias,* "Linus the son (or husband) of Claudia," was the first bishop of Rome after the death of the apostles. But whether this Claudia and Linus should be identified with those mentioned in 2 Timothy is not evident, although it is not improbable. The supposition that Claudia and Linus were mother and son has led some to conclude that she was the wife of Pudens. If so, however, it is then puzzling to explain why their names are separated by that of Linus in the text of 2 Timothy 4:21.

A futher inference which has been made is that the Claudia and Pudens of 2 Timothy were in fact the same Claudia and Pudens mentioned by the Roman poet Martial in his *Epigrams* 4.13 and also identical to some Roman couples similarly named in British (CIL VII.17) and Roman (CIL VI.15,066) inscriptions. But since these names were common, there is no persuasive support for the linking.

In summary, our only reasonable assertion about Claudia is that she was a Christian who knew Paul in Rome and who, because she is mentioned not only with Pudens and Linus, but also with "all the brethren" in sending greetings (4:21) must have been a prominent member of a Roman house church.

Apphia

Apphia, like Claudia, also appears to have been a well-known member of a house church. She is greeted along with others by Paul in his letter to Philemon. Paul opens that short piece of correspondence as follows:

> Paul, a prisoner for Christ Jesus, and Timothy our brother, to Philemon our beloved fellow worker and Apphia our sister and Archippus our fellow soldier, and the church in your house (1–3).

Because this is the sole reference to Apphia in the New Testament, it has been the only source for speculation about her identity. Commentators have closely analyzed her name, some asserting that it was written incorrectly instead of the more familiar Roman name "Appia." Yet, as J. B. Lightfoot has thoroughly documented,[16] the aspirated form "Apphia" has been frequently found on inscriptions from Phrygia where it appears to be a name of native origin.

A Phrygian provenance for Apphia's name is in accord with the widely held opinion that Paul's letter to Philemon, which itself does not identify its recipients' location, was addressed to Christians living in the region of Phrygia, most probably in the small town of Colossae. That conclusion rests in the main on various corresponding links which can be noted between Philemon and the letter to the Colossians (e.g., the Onesimus of Philemon is identified in Colossians 4:9 as being one of the Colossians). Thus, Apphia is likewise considered to have been a Colossian, and the form of her name adds some confirmation to that conclusion.

The question arises as to why Apphia, along with Philemon and Archippus, was singled out for special greeting. Many have assumed she was Philemon's wife or daughter and that Archippus was either their son or her brother.[17] This is related to the supposition, based on the phrase "your house" (Phlm 3), that all three lived in the same household. However, the possessive in this instance is singular in the Greek. That could allow one to conclude that the house referred to is really that of Archippus, although many interpreters nevertheless read the "your" as referring back to Philemon. A tendency then is to see Apphia as having a leadership role in the house church due to its presence in her and her husband's or her father's home.[18] While that may well be a correct analysis, it remains possible that, were the house to be rather that of Archippus, Apphia's being singled out for mention by Paul—and the obvious implication that conveys regarding her importance among the Colossian Christians—must rest on somewhat different grounds than residence in the house.

It is noteworthy that Paul addresses Apphia as "sister" in the same context in which he calls Timothy "brother," Philemon "beloved fellow-worker," and Archippus "fellow-soldier." While the

---

[16]J. B. Lightfoot, *St. Paul's Epistles to the Colossians and to Philemon* (London: Macmillan, 1879, reprinted Grand Rapids: Zondervan, 1978) 306–308.

[17]See Joachim Gnilka, *Der Philemonbrief.* HTKNT X/4 (Freiburg: Herder, 1982) 16.

[18]Cf. Gnilka, *Philemonbrief,* 16: "Sie dürfte durch ihren Mann zum glauben gekommen sein und nimmt jetzt in der Hausgemeinde einen herausragenden Platz sein."

RSV translation given above prefaces each of these appellatives with "our," Norman Petersen has pointed out that in the Greek text Timothy is literally called *ho adelphos,* "the brother" and Apphia *tē adelphē,* "the sister."[19] Paul thus appears to make a distinction between appellatives with which he uses the definite article and those with the possessive pronoun. This is also apparent elsewhere in his writings. For example, in Philippians 2:25 Epaphroditus is identified literally in Greek as *"the* brother and *my* fellow worker and (*my*) fellow soldier."

Petersen argues that in using the definite article rather than the possessive pronoun, Paul focuses on the social positions of brother and sister, not on an individual's relationship with him. He also notes, with many others, that whenever Paul uses the definite article with "brother(s)" or "sister," it generally means that one is a believer. This leads him to conclude that "the brother" or "the sister" is thus "an egalitarian identification applicable to all members of the church, whereas the use of the possessive pronoun has . . . a hierarchical connotation because it links those of whom it is used to *Paul's* position,"[20] e.g., as his fellow-worker or his fellow soldier.

We are consequently left with the impression that in Paul's greeting of Apphia her role as a believer and a community member was foremost in his mind. Paul probably did not single her out because of her relationship to Philemon or Archippus but rather because in his mind she was a faithful or outstanding member, perhaps leader, of the Colossian community whom he happened to know.

Acts and Women Who Must Have Known Paul
The Daughters of Philip,
Mary and Rhoda of Jerusalem

There are a few women in Acts who are not portrayed as having interacted directly with Paul, yet whom we suspect must have known him. These people should be briefly included in our survey insofar as our attempt is to give the broadest possible picture

---

[19]Norman Petersen, *Rediscovering Paul. Philemon and the Sociology of Paul's Narrative World* (Philadelphia: Fortress, 1985) 172, n. 5.

[20]*Ibid.* Italics are his.

of individuals and types of women in touch with Paul. The persons who fall into this group are the daughters of Philip, Mary of Jerusalem, and Mary's servant Rhoda.

The daughters of Philip are mentioned in the New Testament only in the account of Paul's arrival in Caesarea at the end of his third journey:

> On the morrow we departed and came to Caesarea; and we entered the house of Philip the evangelist, who was one of the Seven, and stayed with him. And he had four unmarried daughters, who prophesied (Acts 21:8-9).

The Acts narrative continues by telling the story that the prophet Agabus arrived from Judea and gave a warning to Paul that he would be bound and delivered to the Gentiles in Jerusalem. When "the people there" in Caesarea (21:12) begged Paul not to go on, Paul asked "What are you doing, weeping and breaking my heart?" (21:13).

Interpreters of Acts have been puzzled that while the daughters of Philip are expressly introduced as prophetesses, they make no use of their charism during Paul's encounter with Agabus. Some have supposed Luke's source omitted that they actually did prophesy; others have suggested they were the tearful ones standing by alluded to in the narrative. One proposed resolution of these difficulties is offered by Haenchen. He argues that Luke had an itinerary about Paul which mentioned Philip and his prophesying daughters as Paul's hosts. To this Luke then attached another narrative concerned with prophecy, the details about Agabus.[21]

In any case, Acts would seem to imply an acquaintance between Paul and Philip's daughters. While nothing else about these women is reflected in the New Testament, their ministry itself is referred to and is known to have been highly respected, especially by Paul (in 1 Cor 12:28 to be a prophet is second only to being an apostle; cf. 1 Cor 14:1-5), and not at all an unusual role for women (1 Cor 11:5).[22]

---

[21]Haenchen, *Acts,* 604.

[22]See most recently Antoinette Clark Wire, *The Corinthian Women Prophets. A Reconstruction through Paul's Rhetoric* (Minneapolis: Fortress, 1990).

Tradition holds that Philip the evangelist and his daughters did not remain in Caesarea. Of the numerous strands,[23] one found in Eusebius[24] is that the four women were also prophetesses in Hierapolis in Asia and that their graves as well as their father's were pointed out there toward the end of the second century. Although many recognize some confusion in Eusebius (or his sources) between Philip the apostle and Philip the evangelist, F. F. Bruce's considered opinion judges that this particular Eusebian tradition does apply to the evangelist.[25] Another strand of Christian lore, found in the *Menologion* of Basil, holds that Philip and his daughters moved to Tralles where Philip became bishop.[26] While discussing the reliability of these conflicting traditions would take us too far afield, it is important to note that as a whole they witness to the high regard the early Church had for Philip's daughters.

Besides having known Philip's daughters, Paul, on the basis of information in Acts, must also have been acquainted with Mary of Jerusalem and her servant Rhoda. Mary is introduced in Acts 12:12 as the mother of John Mark and as a person in whose house many Christians gathered together and prayed. Among those who frequented Mary's home were Peter and apparently James (12:12-17). Since Mary's husband is never alluded to, she is thought to have been a widow. She seems to have been well off because she had the resources to host Christian meetings and had at least one servant, Rhoda (12:13). According to Colossians 4:10, Mary's son, John Mark, was the cousin of Barnabas. If so, then Mary must have been his aunt.

From the Acts narrative it is reasonable to suspect that Mary had met Paul personally through both Barnabas and John Mark. For Acts 12:25 associates her son John Mark with Barnabas and Paul following their famine relief trip from Antioch to Jerusalem. Very possibly the two had stayed with Mary and John Mark in Jerusalem during that visit, after which John Mark went off with

---

[23]A detailed summary can be found in Roger Gryson, *The Ministry of Women in the Early Church.* trans. by J. Laporte and M. Hall (Collegeville: The Liturgical Press, 1976) 128, n. 51.

[24]Eusebius, *Ecclesiastical History,* III, xxx. 3-4.

[25]F. F. Bruce, *The Epistles to the Colossians, to Philemon, and to the Ephesians.* NICNT (Grand Rapids: Eerdmans, 1984) 16.

[26]Basil, *Menologion,* I.111 (*PG,* CXVII, 103).

them to Antioch (12:25). Presumably Mary's servant Rhoda, who knew Peter well (12:14-17), also had met Paul if he stayed in Mary's household. While nothing is known of her, William Ramsay once mused that she must have been "in the most real sense a part of the household, fully sharing in the anxieties and the joys of the family, knowing the family's friends as her own friends."[27]

The disparate group of people in this chapter, about whom there is little to piece together, nevertheless add to our survey fifteen more women who knew, or at least knew of, Paul. Each, in spite of how little the existing sources witness to her, rightfully has her niche in the history of the early Church. Each also takes her place in our overview not only as an individual but as an example of roles held by women or types of women who knew Paul. These people remind us that women interacted with Paul whom he recognized as workers in the Lord, some who were sisters in Christian community, others who had shown him hospitality, servants in households where he had stayed, and women who prophesied. When these women are viewed along with all those already described in our earlier chapters, it is undeniable that many different individuals and types of women had experienced Paul as part of their lives. But, all the people we have surveyed up to this point have been either members of Paul's family or attached in some sense to his Churches. A dimension of women's acquaintance with Paul that we know almost nothing about are those who encountered him outside those spheres. There are two such women who are purported to have known Paul and thus it is to them that our attention now turns.

[27]See the chapter "Rhoda the Slave Girl," in his *The Bearing of Recent Discovery on the Trustworthiness of the New Testament* (London: Hodder and Stoughton, 4th ed. 1920) 209-222, 210.

7

Women of the Jewish Aristocracy:
Bernice and Drusilla

According to the Acts narrative, two aristocratic women, Bernice and Drusilla, had occasion to meet Paul. Both were the great grand-daughters of Herod the Great and the daughters of Herod Agrippa I and his wife, Cypros. Before describing the lives of Bernice and Drusilla and their encounters with Paul, it is interesting to recall some background information about their father.

Agrippa I lived many years in Rome and was a friend of the Emperors Caligula and Claudius. He was made king over Philip's tetrarchy in 37, over that of Antipas in 40, and over all Judea in 41. From 41 Agrippa I ruled all of that territory until his sudden death at Caesarea in 44 (cf. Acts 12:19-23).

While Agrippa I had lived a wild existence before taking political power, he presented himself in office quite differently. As king he was careful to carry out the observances of Judaism and thereby to gain the respect of the Pharisees. Thus, under his regime Pharisaism flourished. Josephus reports that Agrippa "enjoyed residing in Jerusalem and did so constantly; and he scrupulously observed the traditions of his people. He neglected no rite of purification, and no day passed for him without the prescribed sacrifice."[1] Agrippa's motivation, however, was not religious fervor but political acumen. His concern was to have the approval of the people, who were for the most part led by the Pharisees. In his attempt to please the Jews, for example, Agrippa had James the son of Zebedee killed and Peter arrested (Acts 12:1-5).

[1]Josephus, *Antiquities* XIX, 331.

Agrippa's strategy of religious observance for the purpose of political advantage was no doubt conveyed to his son Agrippa II and to his daughters, Bernice, Mariamme, and Drusilla. Drusilla and Bernice are briefly mentioned in Acts because of meetings they had with Paul in Caesarea in about 58 and 60 respectively. Because more information can be compiled about Bernice, mainly from Josephus, her life will be described first.[2]

Bernice

Born in 28, Bernice was first married to Marcus Julius Alexander, son of Alexander Lysimachus, a Jewish official (alabarch) in Alexandria who was a brother of Philo.[3] After Marcus died, Agrippa I gave Bernice in marriage to her uncle, his elder brother Herod of Chalcis, by whom she had two sons, Berenicianus and Hyrcanus. Herod of Chalcis died in 48, and Bernice then lived for many years as a widow. Eventually, however, it was rumored that she had become incestuously involved with her brother, Agrippa II.[4] The rumor, while it may have been based on fact, could also have gained currency because Bernice presided over the court of Agrippa II, and he had never married. Whatever the case, to quell the controversy Bernice induced Polemo, the king of Cilicia, to marry her in 64. Polemo was persuaded chiefly on account of Bernice's wealth.[5] The marriage required him to become a Jewish proselyte, but when Bernice deserted him, in the words of Josephus, "out of licentiousness," Polemo was "relieved simultaneously of his marriage and of further adherence to the Jewish way of life."[6] Upon leaving Polemo, Bernice returned to live again with Agrippa II and continued to play an important role in his reign. Her significance is reflected in the appearance of her name on various inscriptions, on some of which Bernice's name even precedes Agrippa II's, due to the fact that by her mar-

---

[2]For a photograph of a bust of Bernice found in Herculaneum and now on display in the National Museum, Rome, see Gaalya Cornfeld (gen. ed.), *Josephus. The Jewish War* (Grand Rapids: Zondervan, 1982) 174.

[3]So Josephus, *Antiquities* XIX, 277.

[4]So *ibid.*, XX, 146-147.

[5]So *ibid.*, XX, 145-146.

[6]*Ibid.*, XX, 146.

riage to Herod of Chalcis she had achieved royal rank before her brother.[7]

Agrippa II did not rule as much territory as had his father. When the elder Agrippa died in 44, Agrippa II was only seventeen and therefore Claudius did not immediately allow him to rule. By 50, however, he was given the small territory of Herod of Chalcis, which in 53 he exchanged for what had been the tetrarchy of Philip and various territories in Lebanon. Nero later added parts of Galilee and Perea to Agrippa's domain, and Agrippa therefore renamed his capital, Caesarea Philippi, Neronia to honor the emperor. Agrippa also controlled the investment of the high priest in Jerusalem and served the Romans as an important confidant in Jewish matters.

It is in the latter role that Agrippa and Bernice are found when, according to Acts 25–26, they meet the Apostle Paul. The event is generally dated about 60, thus before Bernice's marriage to Polemo and during the period in which she was first living with her brother. The details in Acts of the encounter appear to derive more from the author's creativity and literary purposes than from any historical meeting,[8] although the probability that Bernice and Agrippa made a trip to Caesarea to welcome Festus does allow for an encounter with Paul. But even in the event of total fabrication by the author of Acts, such political figures as Bernice and Agrippa nevertheless were people of whom Paul would have been well aware. And, conversely, followers of Jesus such as Paul, although perhaps not known individually, could hardly have escaped the attention of the royal pair as they dealt with controversial issues among their fellow Jewish subjects. Thus their alleged examination of Paul is pertinent to our interest in those women who knew Paul. Bernice is an example of the type of woman who would have been politically, and maybe religiously, concerned with him.

As Acts portrays the scene, Bernice and Agrippa had gone to Caesarea (in 60) to welcome the new Roman procurator Festus. While there, Festus consulted Agrippa about the case of the prisoner Paul, whom his predecessor Felix had turned over to him.

[7]See Michael Grant, *The Jews in the Roman World* (New York: Charles Scribner's Sons, 1973) 159.

[8]So Haenchen, *Acts,* 677–79.

Paul had already refused a trial in Jerusalem and then appealed to Festus "to be kept in custody for the decision of the emperor" (25:21). Agrippa requested a hearing with Paul, at which he and Bernice arrived "with great pomp," attended by "military tribunes and the prominent men of the city" (25:21). The interview was dominated by Paul, whose impassioned defense left Festus, Agrippa, and Bernice to conclude that he had done "nothing to deserve death or imprisonment" (26:31).

For those who were familiar with the lives of Agrippa and Bernice, as no doubt the recipients of Acts must have been, there is an implicit poignancy in the scene. Paul explains Jewish hostility toward himself as rooted in his preaching to both Jews and Gentiles "that they should repent and turn to God and perform deeds worthy of their repentance" (26:20). One suspects that Agrippa and Bernice, as in the Acts story, had heard such a moral challenge to themselves perhaps numerous times. What had been their reaction? Were they resentful or just oblivious about criticism? While there is little to relate to answering those questions, the author of Acts does appear to have had no tradition of hostility on the part of Bernice and Agrippa toward Christians in general, in contrast, for example, to what he passes on about their father (cf. 12:1-5). But this is an observation based on silence and therefore not necessarily a compelling one.

The years of Bernice's life following this supposed encounter with Paul in ca. 60 were filled with much tumult as events led up to the Jewish War of 66–70. During the term of Gessius Florus (64–66), the last procurator of Judea, violent opposition among the Jews was aroused by his cruelty and avarice. Bernice, once when she was in Jerusalem, witnessed certain murderous outrages committed by the Roman soldiers and implored Florus to put a stop to the carnage. But he, "regarding neither the number of the slaves nor the exalted rank of his suppliant, but only the profit accruing from the plunder, turned a deaf ear to her prayers."[9] Bernice was in Jerusalem at the time to observe a Nazirite vow (cf. Acts 21:23-26), although her reason for undergoing such a ritual of purification is not known. Josephus reports that during her Nazirite period "she would come barefoot before the tribunal

---

[9]Josephus, *Jewish War* II, 311.

and make supplication to Florus, without any respect being shown to her, even at the peril of her life.''[10]

While Bernice and Agrippa attempted as far as possible to support the Jews, their true loyalty was to Rome, and this never wavered. After they were unable to prevent the Jewish revolt in 66, Agrippa and Bernice joined the Romans. They became closely associated first with Vespasian and then with his son and successor Titus, the conqueror of Jerusalem. Bernice herself became the mistress of Titus during the war. Later, in 75, she and Agrippa were invited to live in his palace in Rome when Vespasian was emperor. Agrippa was even appointed *praetor*. However, well-known Cynics made fun of Titus' infatuation with Bernice, fifteen years his senior, and while these Cynics were consequently executed, Titus against his will sent Bernice and Agrippa back home.[11]

In 79, when Titus became emperor himself, Bernice returned to Rome fully expecting to become his wife, only to be rejected again for Titus immediately obeyed the wishes of the senatorial party and rejected her request for marriage.[12] The idea of such a marriage between the emperor and a foreigner was repugnant to the Romans.

There is an extremely rare Palestinian coin issued in about 79–80 under Agrippa which may be related to this incident. On the obverse the coin pictures a veiled woman as the emperor's wife; the reverse shows an anchor. It has been theorized that this coin was actually issued in anticipation of Bernice's marriage to Titus and her elevation to the status of the *Sebastē,* the emperor's wife, with the anchor referring to her sea voyage to Rome.[13] However, an important argument against this interpretation of the coin is that it celebrates an event which had not yet occurred. It would seem to have been a case of extreme audacity to call Bernice empress before the fact. Nevertheless, this may indeed have been what happened, with the coin's rarity indicating its removal from circulation because of the embarassment to everyone concerned.

---

[10]*Ibid.,* II, 314.

[11]So Suetonius, *The Lives of the Twelve Caesars: Titus,* 7.1; Dio Cassius, *History* 65.15.3b-6.

[12]Suetonius, *The Lives of the Twelve Caesars: Titus* 7.1; Dio Cassius, *History* 66.18.1.

[13]See Jacob Maltiel-Gerstenfeld, "A Portrait Coin of Berenice Sister of Agrippa II?" *Israel Numismatic Journal* 4 (1980) 25–26.

After her final rejection by Titus, Bernice returned to Palestine where she presumably spent the latter years of her life. While there is nothing further to add to her story, there is an anecdote about Titus which Bernice may have heard with much interest. As Suetonius reports the tale, when Titus lay dying of a fever in 81 at the young age of 42, he "complained bitterly that life was being undeservedly taken from him—since only a single sin lay on his conscience."[14] Although at the time some interpreted this to refer to the affair he had had with his brother's wife Domitia,[15] or offered various other theories,[16] some Jews said he was regretting his impious entry into the forbidden Holy of Holies in the Jerusalem Temple during the Jewish War. And indeed, Titus had probably been reproached for that act by Bernice as well as other Jews. It is not impossible, therefore, that he died haunted by the memory of their disapproval. One wonders if Bernice would have felt some vindication as she heard such a report. These musings cannot be carried further, however, since they rest on mere speculation.

With respect to our interest in Bernice's acquaintance with Paul, it appears in reviewing her life that her encounter with Paul, or the other believers like him of whom she surely was aware, had little lasting meaning for her. This is a quite different reaction to the Apostle than we have observed in various other women who knew him. Bernice, and Drusilla also as will be evident below, thus serves to illustrate that some women who met Paul either rejected or were simply untouched by his message.

Drusilla

Bernice and Agrippa II's younger sister Drusilla was born about 38 C.E. Her father Agrippa I had arranged with Antiochus Epiphanes, son of King Antiochus of Commagene, to marry her. But he had withdrawn from the contract, being unwilling to convert to Judaism. Therefore, in about 53 Drusilla's brother Agrippa

---

[14]Suetonius, *The Lives of the Twelves Caesars: Titus,* 10.

[15]See *ibid.,* 10.

[16]See Michael Grant, *The Roman Emperors* (New York: Charles Scribners Sons, 1985) 59.

II gave her in marriage to Azizus, king of Emesa in Syria.[17] He agreed to be circumcised to contract the marriage.

Drusilla's marriage to Azizus did not last long, due to the following circumstances. Antonius Felix, the Roman procurator of Judea from 52–60, at the time married to another Drusilla, the grand-daughter of Antony and Cleopatra, saw the Jewish Drusilla and "conceived a passion for the lady."[18] Felix sent to her a Cyprian Jew named Atomus, who pretended to be a magician in hopes of persuading her to leave Azizus and marry Felix. Atomus promised that Felix would make her "supremely happy"[19] if she did not reject his proposal. (There may be a play here on the meaning of the Latin *felix,* "happy.") Drusilla, unhappy and wanting to be distanced from her sister Bernice's jealousy of her beauty, agreed to transgress Jewish law and marry Felix.[20] That Agrippa II allowed his sister to marry the Roman official without the usual requirement of circumcision is a sign that he must have viewed the match as advantageous, and indeed, it appears to have contributed to friendly relationships between the Romans and the Jews in the early years of the procuratorship of Felix.

Drusilla had a son by Felix whom she named Agrippa. Josephus records that this son and his wife disappeared in 79 at the time of the eruption of Mount Vesuvius, but no further details are given.[21] It is possible that Drusilla herself also died in that eruption,[22] since after Felix was removed from office in 60 (due to immorality and incompetence), they assumably moved to Italy.

Drusilla had occasion to meet Paul even before his supposed meeting with Bernice. Acts 24:24 indicates that Drusilla was with Felix in about 58 on one occasion when he had sent for the imprisoned Paul. The narrative stresses that Drusilla was present, although it is not clear whether she went at her own request or was invited by Felix because she was a Jewess (24:24). The pas-

---

[17]So Josephus, *Antiquities* XX, 139–140.

[18]*Ibid.,* 142.

[19]*Ibid.* Some manuscripts call this person Simon rather than Atomus.

[20]So *ibid.* XX, 143.

[21]See *ibid.* XX, 143–144.

[22]Haenchen, 660.

sage also attributes to Felix, even though he was not a Jew, "a rather accurate knowledge of the Way" (22:22).[23]

According to Acts, Paul spoke about "faith in Christ Jesus" (24:24) and "argued about justice and self-control and future judgment" (24:25). While Felix is said to have become alarmed, no account of Drusilla's reaction is given. The incident concludes by noting that Felix held Paul for two years, and that when his term as procurator ended, "desiring to do the Jews a favor" (24:27), he left Paul in prison.[24]

From what is known about the lives and personalities of Drusilla and Bernice, it appears that neither had more than a passing interest in Paul or others like him nor in the message they preached. To these women one suspects that Paul would have been just one more Jew who claimed that a Messiah had come. He was one more of the followers of Jesus upsetting the Jerusalem establishment whom the royalty were concerned to humor. For members of the Jewish aristocracy such as these women, who were overtly Jewish primarily out of political expedience, wealth, power, and cooperation with the dominating Romans left little reason to need or hope for a Messiah, and no concern with claims made that one had arrived—other than the threat to the aristocracy's power such a figure might pose. Thus, for the likes of Bernice and Drusilla, the likes of Paul would probably have seemed little more than curious, disruptive characters. The meetings of these women with Paul evidently made no great impression upon them even though a moral challenge seems to have been an element of their encounters (cf. Acts 24:25, 26:20). The criticism of his hearers' lives implicit in Paul's defense of himself and in his preaching brought an element of confrontation into his conversations with members of the royalty. One recognizes in these episodes echoes of the encounter of John the Baptist with Herod Antipas and Herodias in the Synoptic tradition (cf. Mark 6:14-29; Matt 14:1-12; Luke 9:7-9).

[23]The Western text elaborates on the incident with a variant phrase which indicates that Drusilla wanted to see Paul, and so Felix had summoned him to please her.

[24]The Western text again has a variant reading which replaces this expressed consideration for the Jews with concern for Drusilla, the implication being that she had taken offense at Paul's speech.

In summary, there is nothing to suggest in what we know of the lives of Bernice and Drusilla that Paul's implicit but forthright challenge to them was felt as more than a passing sting. Paul, or in the event he did not historically meet these women, the message he represented, did not meet with lasting receptivity in their lives. Perhaps Paul was unnerving to them for a short time, but ultimately he had no evident impact.

In our survey of women who knew Paul, it is interesting to have come across two for whom he held little significance. This contrasts with what we have seen concerning other women, most of whom probably respected and revered Paul, for some of whom he had been a close associate or an instrument of profound conversion. Bernice and Drusilla thus serve to extend our spectrum of women who knew Paul to range now from those who owed him their very conversions to those who in effect dismissed him. Along that spectrum we have met a variety of individuals and types. They are but the tip of the iceberg of the women in Paul's world of early Christianity.

Summary:
A Memorial Past Forgetting

"How would you like your epitaph to read?" When confronted by this question, we feel challenged to reduce our life to a short, pithy statement. Envisioning future generations who might gaze on our grave markers knowing nothing else about us, we suggest a few short phrases which convey the most essential.

Epitaphs come to mind as one studies the women in early Christianity. Their memory in tradition often rests on no more than a phrase or a sentence or two in a New Testament document. Unfortunately, the small bits of information passed on are sometimes not those central identity traits so selectively put into real epitaphs. Instead, New Testament women are largely accidentally, or better, incidentally memorialized. The one-line places of many of these women in the documents of Christian origins often function not to summarize their lives, but to relate them to someone else's story or concerns, for example, Paul's.

The women we have encountered have emerged as a diverse, lively, vibrant group of people who intrigue us as we reach across the centuries to them in their political, cultural, social, and religious situations so different from our own. Surely Paul would be the first to welcome all attempts to portray these women in their own right since for many of them, especially those who were Christians, he expressed praise and gratitude. In this respect, it is interesting that Eusebius in his fourth-century *Ecclesiastical His-*

tory offered this observation about all the persons who had collaborated with Paul, thus including most of the women we have
discussed:

> There were many thousands of his fellow-workers and, as he
> called them himself, fellow-soldiers, of whom most were granted
> by him memorial past forgetting, for he recounts his testimony
> to them unceasingly in his own letters, and, moreover, Luke
> also in Acts gives a list of those known to him and mentions
> them by name.[1]

Although Eusebius is undoubtedly exaggerating the number of
Paul's co-workers, he is right on target in describing the result
of Paul's and Luke's (and other New Testament authors') mention of them: they have been memorialized past forgetting. And,
indeed, this is true for every man or woman, saint or sinner, whose
name entered the pages of Scripture, however inadvertently. Thus
recorded, their memory has been preserved.

Yet that memorial as far as some of the women who knew Paul
are concerned has been perpetuated only in the midst of much
struggle. As we have seen, a few women's names have been removed from some manuscripts of the New Testament, the gender
of others has been disputed, and the roles and work of still others
have been denied or diminished at the hands of various translators and commentators. As a result, today much scholarly energy
is being spent not only on preserving the memory of the women
who knew Paul but on recovering more fully than ever before
their stories and those of other early Christian women. This survey has presented an introductory overview of these people and
one gateway into their world. The thirty some women we have
scrutinized have offered us a partial cross section of the women
who would have known such a pivotal early Christian as Paul.
And they have thus represented for us the broader spectrum of
some of the types of women whose lives peopled the era of the
nascent Church.

We began by looking at Paul's mother and sister, and his possible wife. As obscure as these individuals remain, they nevertheless remind us that there were women whose lives had been closely

---

[1]*Ecclesiastical History* III, iv. 4–5.

bonded to Paul in his earlier years and thus may have been greatly affected emotionally, spiritually, perhaps even economically, by his profound conversion and itinerancy. The study then moved on to women remembered especially for their faith, all apparently converts of Paul. Of these, Lois and Eunice present examples of Hellenistic Jewish women converts from Asia Minor, some of whom like Eunice were in socially difficult marriages to a Gentile. Damaris the Athenian, in contrast, also brought to faith by Paul, hints at a different type of Christian convert, Gentile women from large, highly cultural cities.

In turning to Lydia, Chloe, and Nympha, we met the household head, business woman type of person who knew Paul, some of whom became Christians and offered hospitality and leadership to the Christian cells he founded. Next examined were those whom Paul specifically called co-workers, Euodia, Syntyche, and Prisca. In the midst of their individuality and very different life experiences these three taken together suggest that strong, apparently very forthright personalities, not unlike Paul's own, were among those who worked compatibly with him. Thereafter followed an examination of the deacon, Phoebe, and the apostle Junia, people whose lives attest to the presence of women in such significant roles or ministries in the early Churches.

Our overview next looked at various members of the Roman house churches (besides Prisca), first those Paul had described as workers in the Lord, Mary, Tryphaena, Tryphosa, and Persis, and then certain other Church members, some in Rome such as the mother of Rufus, Julia, the sister of Nereus, and Claudia, and one in the region of Colossae, Apphia. Also brought in for some consideration were various women mentioned in Acts who presumably had to have known Paul, the prophetesses who were daughters of Philip, Mary of Jerusalem, and her slave girl Rhoda. Our survey concluded by looking at Bernice and Drusilla, who, unlike all of the above, were acquainted with Paul neither as family nor through his Churches, but as figures significant in the politics of the day. With these two women we encountered a type of wealthy, aristocratic woman for whom Paul and his message appeared to have had little impact.

In retrospect, we have examined a wide array of individuals and constructed partial sketches of whatever aspects of their lives the New Testament texts, other sources, and scholarly discussion have opened the way to pursue. The portrayals which have resulted are necessarily fragmentary and uneven. Yet even becoming more conversant with these individuals via a few dimensions of their lives helps to draw us into the world of New Testament women. And, insofar as some of these individuals have also suggested rather general types of women in the milieu of early Christianity, they help us to envision more of those who remain totally unknown.

While our point of departure has been primarily New Testament references to the women who knew Paul, other sources of information, especially archaeological, have occasionally been cited to illuminate their spheres of activity. Yet, a vast array of other avenues of study and sources concerning the ancient world exists which need to be considered for a better understanding of these women. The data we have discussed about them suggest numerous questions which deserve further attention. For example, what could we learn about women and travel, women and education, women and law, women as missionaries or leaders of religious groups outside Judaism or Christianity? What were houses and house churches like? What did women do in their households? What did slave women do? And so on. . . . The list of questions seems endless; the scholarly tasks appear formidable. Significant advances have already been made, however, by many writers, numerous of whom have been cited throughout this book. Nevertheless, a vast amount could still be done.[2]

The women who knew Paul, who have been memorialized past forgetting in the New Testament, are indeed committed to Christianity's collective memory. But they have also experienced much relegation to obscurity. We will probably never know as much about Lydia, Prisca, Phoebe, Junia, and the others as we do about Paul. On the other hand, we will also never truly know Paul until these women's stories can be told more fully.

---

[2]Brooten's "Early Christian Women," *passim,* offers an excellent survey of the general state of the research.

Further Reading

Bernadette Brooten, "Early Christian Women and Their Cultural Context: Issues of Method in Historical Reconstruction," in Adela Yarbro Collins (ed.), *Feminist Perspectives on Biblical Scholarship*. SBL Centennial Publications 10, Chico, CA: Scholars Press, 1985, 65–91.

F. F. Bruce, *The Pauline Circle*. Grand Rapids: Eerdmans, 1985.

Elisabeth Schüssler Fiorenza, *In Memory of Her*. New York: Crossroad, 1983.

Wayne Meeks, *The First Urban Christians. The Social World of the Apostle Paul*. New Haven: Yale University Press, 1983.

Ben Witherington, *Women in the Earliest Churches*. Society for New Testament Studies Monograph Series 8, Cambridge: Cambridge University Press, 1988.